SUSTAINABLE DEVELOPMENT GOALS FOR THE VULNERABLE IN INDIA

About the Authors

Bedprakas Syam Roy did his MA in Economics in 1968 from the Calcutta University and Ph.D. from the North Bengal University in 1987. He started his career in the West Bengal Civil Service (1970) and was then selected in the IAS (1989). He is specialised in development administration, decentralised planning and state planning. After retirement, he served as Member of the Third State Finance Commission, West Bengal. He authored ten books and several articles.

Maniparna Syam Roy did her M.Sc. in Economics from Calcutta University in 2003 (through Presidency College, Kolkata) and Ph.D. in Economics from Jadavpur University in 2011; Topic of Research: Accounting for Air and Water Resources: A Case Study of West Bengal. She has been Assistant Professor of Economics in Asutosh College, Kolkata from 12.9.2008 till date and was also a Guest faculty of the Department of Economics, University of Calcutta for six years.

SUSTAINABLE DEVELOPMENT GOALS FOR THE VULNERABLE IN INDIA

B.P. Syam Roy
Maniparna Syam Roy

CONCEPT PUBLISHING COMPANY PVT. LTD.
NEW DELHI - 110059

ISBN: 978-93-5594-657-7

First Published 2024

Published and Printed by

Concept Since 1974

Concept Publishing Company Pvt. Ltd.
A/15-16, Commercial Block, Mohan Garden
New Delhi-110059 (India)
T: +91-11-41101460
E: publishing@conceptpub.com, *W*: www.conceptpub.com

Cataloging in Publication--Courtesy: D.K. Agencies (P) Ltd. <docinfo@dkagencies.com>

Shyamroy, Bedprakash, author.
Sustainable development goals for the vulnerable in India / B.P. Syam Roy, Maniparna Syam Roy.
pages cm
Includes bibliographical references and index.
ISBN 9789355946577

1. Sustainable development--India. 2. People with disabilities--Services for--India. 3. India--Economic policy. 4. India--Social policy. I. Syam Roy, Maniparna, author. II. Title.

LCC HC440.E5S59 2024 | DDC 338.9270954 23

Preface

The concept of sustainable development owes its origin to balanced use of stock of resources. Brundtland defined in 'Our Common Future' as that *development that meets the needs of the present without compromising the ability of future generations to meet their own needs.* It is intended to meet Humanity's quest for a fairly equitable quality life 'For All' not as one-off affair or transient in nature but to have a reasonable foundation of strength of continuity in a sustainable manner. The concept of sustainability is the central pillar to the new approach to development. Sustainable development has three dimensions, domains or pillars, namely "economic, environmental and social" or "ecology, economy and equity" while some scholars include a fourth pillar, namely culture, institutions or governance.

The UN Sustainable Development Summit in September, 2015 broadened and fine-tuned the core of Sustainable Development that calls for concerted efforts towards building an inclusive, sustainable and resilient future for people and planet. The historical declaration also insists that to this journey of sustainable development, nobody shall be left behind and calls for special efforts for the vulnerable who very often escapes the development radar.

The present exercise is a joint study of Dr. Maniparna Syam Roy and myself of the way in which the vulnerable could be meaningfully integrated with the sustainable development process, and achieve the ends of related sustainable development goals. Apart from writing the chapters on Person with disabilities and Scheduled

Tribes, Dr. Syam Roy has contributed meaningfully to the structural design of the study and the issues governing the vulnerable, apart from revising the draft. Besides, she has been constant source of inspiration and assistance to complete the manuscripts in time.

In undertaking this Study, I have made extensive use of related publications from the websites of different Ministries, Government of India and NITI Aayog. I have also made substantial use of materials from the websites of the UN system and multiple partners working on Sustainable development goals including Sustainable Development Summit Conference, Sustainable Development Knowledge platform, the World Bank and also of numerous others for making liberal use of relevant materials to prepare the book.

Finally, I acknowledge the assistance that I received from Shri Ashok K. Mittal, publishing editor of the Concept, to publish the book at the quickest possible time.

Saltlake, **Dr. Bedprakas Syam Roy**
2nd April, 2023 bpsyamroy@yahoo.co.in

Contents

Acronyms

ABHWC	: Ayushman Bharat—Health and Wellness Centres
AGY	: (Sansad) Adarsh Gram Yojana
BBBP	: Beti Bachao Beti Padhao Scheme (BBBP)
BPL	: Below the Poverty Level
CDI	: Child Development Index
CDM	: Clean Development Mechanism
CO_2	: Carbon dioxide
Covid-19	: Coronavirus disease of 2019
CWMSrC	: Welfare Schemes for Senior Citizens
DMC	: Domestic material consumption
FDI	: Foreign Direct Investment
FGM	: Female genital mutilation
GB	: Gender Budget
GCF	: Green Climate Fund
GDP	: Gross domestic product
GGGR	: Global Gender Gap Report (GGGR) of the World Economic Forum (WEF)
GHG	: Greenhouse gas
GNI	: Gross National Income
GRB	: Gender Responsive Budget
HIV	: Human Immunodeficiency Virus
HLPF	: (United Nations) High-level Political Forum
ICTs	: Information and Communication Technologies
ILO	: International Labour Organisation

IMR	: Infant Mortality Rate
IPC	: Indian Penal Code
JAM	: Jandhan Aadhaar Mobile
JSSK	: Janani Shishu Suraksha Karyakram
JSY	: Janani Suraksha Yojana
KBA	: Key Biodiversity Areas
KGBP	: Kasturba Gandhi Balika Vidyalaya
MDGS	: Millennium Development Goals
MMR	: Maternal Mortality Rate (MMR)
MNREGS	: Mahatma Gandhi National Rural Employment Guarantee Scheme
MoEF	: Ministry of Environment, Forest & Environment
MSK	: Mahila Shakti Kendras
NCPCR	: National Commission for Protection of Child Rights
NEET	: National Education, Employment or Training
NFHS-5	: National Family Welfare and Health Survey-5
NGO	: Non Government Organisations
NGREGS	: National Employment Guarantee Scheme
NIPEP	: National Institute of Public Finance and Policy
NITI Aayog	: National Institution for Transforming India
NISD	: National Institute of Social Defence.
NPOP	: National Policy on Older Persons
N_2O	: Nitrous Oxide
ODA	: Official development assistance
OSC	: One Stop Centre Scheme
PESA	: Panchayats (Extension to the Scheduled Areas) Act
PM 2.5	: Particulate matter
PMSMA	: Pradhan Mantri Surakshit Matritva Abhiyan
POSCO Act	: Protection of Children from Sexual Offences (POCSO) Act, 2012
PPM	: parts per million
PVTG	: Particularly Vulnerable Tribal Groups
PWD	: Persons with Disabilities

RRTC : Regional Resources & Training Centres
RVY : Rashtriya Vayoshri Yajona
SAARC : South Asian Association for Regional Cooperation
SAPSrC) : State Action Plan for Senior Citizens
SC&ST : Scheduled Castes & Scheduled Tribes
SCPCR : State Commission for Protection of Child Rights
SDGs : Sustainable Development Goals
SDG Report : Sustainable Development Goals Report
SRS : Sample Registration System
STEPW : Support to Training and Employment Programmes for Women
SUMAN : Surakshit Matritva Aashwasan Scheme
TSP : Tribal Sub-Plan
UGC : University Grant Commission
UK : United Kingdom
UNDP : United Nations Development Programme
UNEP : United Nations Environmental Programme
UNESCO : United Nations Educational, Scientific and Cultural Organization
UNFCCC : United Nations Framework Convention on Climatic Change
UNICEF : United Nations International Children's Emergency Fund
UNSDG Report, 2020 : United Nations Sustainable Development Goals Report, 2020
USD : United States Dollar
UT : Union Territories
VNR : Voluntary National Review
WCD : Ministry of Women & Child Development
WHO : World Health Organization
WMO : World Meteorological Organization
WSSD : World Summit on Sustainable Development

1
An Overview of the Current Status of Sustainable Development Goals

The declaration of Sustainable Development Summit, 2015 of the new agenda of development for the humanity contained a comprehensive, far-reaching and people-centred set of universal and transformative Goals and Targets for the full implementation of the Sustainable Development Goals by 2030 for eradicating poverty in all its forms and dimensions, and achieving sustainable development in its three dimensions—economic, social and environmental—in a balanced and integrated manner. Built upon the achievements of the MDGs, the new SDGs are set to address its unfinished agenda and go beyond to address comprehensively five focus areas, people, planet, prosperity, peace and partnership through 17-SDGs. The new development agenda became operational from First January, 2016. The Summit also declared systemic follow-up and review of the implementation of the Agenda for the next 15 years. Consequently, the Sustainable Development Goals Reports depicting the global and country level achievements have continued to be published annually indicating the gap areas, goal-wise, to be bridged during the implementation journey. Right up to this point, seven Sustainable Development Goals Reports (2016 to 2022) have since been published, the Sustainable Development Goals Report, 2022 being the latest.

The implementation journey of the sustainable development goals around the world took off with great enthusiasm with varying degree of achievements right up to 2019. However, with the coming into coronavirus, the momentum of progress got adversely affected and for the second year in a row, the world is no longer making perceptible progress on the SDGs. The Sustainable Development Goals Report 2022 provides the global overview of progress on the implementation of the 2030 Agenda for Sustainable Development, based on the latest available data and estimates. It also tracks the global and regional progress towards the 17 Goals with in-depth analyses of selected indicators for each Goal, a brief summary of which is captured hereunder.

Goal 1: End Poverty in All its Forms Everywhere

Global poverty continued its historical decline between 2015 and 2018 with the extreme poverty rate falling from 10.1 per cent to 8.6 per cent. As a result, the number of people living on less than $1.90 a day dropped from 740 million to 656 million over this period. The COVID-19 has made a severe dent in that progress and as per estimates, the global poverty rate increased sharply from 2019 to 2020, from 8.3 per cent to 9.2 per cent, thus erasing more than four years of steady gains. It effectively means that an additional 93 million people worldwide were pushed into extreme poverty because of the pandemic. The efforts to catch-up pre-Covid trend has yet to bear any positive result and an estimated 75 million more people than expected prior to the pandemic will be living in extreme poverty. The said Report also mentions that in 2020, the share of workers living in extreme poverty rose for the first time in two decades and over half of the unemployed in high-income countries receive cash benefits compared with 1 per cent in low-income countries. Similarly, only 28.9 per cent of people considered vulnerable—all children, along with older people and those of working age not covered by social insurance—had access to social assistance cash benefits in 2020, with coverage varying widely across regions. Sixty-three per cent of those considered vulnerable in high-income countries received cash benefits compared with just 7.8 per cent in low-income countries.

SDG 2: End Hunger, Achieve Food Security and Improved Nutrition and Promote Sustainable Agriculture

The world faces severe food crisis with a rising number of people experiencing hunger and food insecurity by a combination of growing conflicts, climate related shocks and widening inequalities. Consequently, an estimated 828 million people have suffered from hunger in 2021. The impact of war in Ukraine poses an additional threat to food insecurity, levels of hunger and malnutrition, especially among the poorest and most vulnerable. Further, Conflict, COVID-19, climate change and growing inequalities are converging to undermine food security worldwide. The low labour productivity of small-scale food producers remains also a big concern area. Additionally, pandemic and growing food insecurity have dented further the slow progress on child malnutrition. The proportion of countries affected by high food prices increased sharply in 2020.

Goal 3: Ensure Healthy Lives and Promote Well-Being for All at All Ages

The COVID-19 continues to affect Sustainable Development Goal 3 targets of ensuring people's health and well-being globally. Up to 2018, substantial progress could be achieved in many areas of health, including reproductive, maternal and child health, immunization coverage and treatment of communicable diseases despite huge regional disparities. As of mid-2022, COVID-19 had infected more than 500 million people worldwide and disrupted essential health services, and halted two decades of work towards making health coverage universal. As a result, immunization coverage dropped for the first time in 10 years. For the record, COVID-19 directly and indirectly led to the deaths of nearly 15 million people in the first two years of the pandemic. The pandemic has also triggered a significant rise in anxiety and depression, particularly among young people. The health and economic impacts of COVID-19 have worsened uneven progress towards universal health coverage. Widespread disruptions have derailed progress against HIV, tuberculosis and malaria. The vaccine programme of the children are particularly affected. From 2019 to 2020, coverage of infant immunization slipped from 86 to 83 per cent. This means that 22.7 million children missed out on vaccinations in 2020, 3.7 million more than in 2019 and the highest number since 2005. In addition, 17.1 million older children did not receive vaccines through the routine immunization programme in 2020, an increase from 13.6 million in 2019.The COVID-19 pandemic has also taken a heavy toll on health and care workers, who are already stretched thin in most regions.

Goal 4: Ensure Inclusive and Equitable Quality Education and Promote Lifelong Learning Opportunities for All

The crisis in education has deepened with severe disruptions during COVID-19. It brought about worrisome consequences in School closures and children's learning particularly for girls and those who are disadvantaged, including children with disabilities, rural dwellers and ethnic minorities. It is estimated that about147 million children missed more than half of their in-person instruction over the past two years. Before the pandemic, 17 per cent of children and youth globally were out of primary and secondary school; however, this figure rose to 26 per cent in 2020. It is noted that from March 2020 to February 2022, worldwide schools remained fully or partially closed for 41 weeks, on average. Such prolonged school closures have heightened the risk that a section of children is not likely to return to school. Further, it has also cast a shadow on a dire picture of learning outcomes. Additionally, entrenched inequities in education have worsened during the pandemic. School closures during the pandemic have particularly deepened inequality in education and the marginalized populations most affected. In pursuit of zeal of uniform learning outcomes, such vulnerable students need adequate psychological support when schools are functional.

Goal 5: Achieve Gender Equality and Empower all Women and Girls

The SDG Report, 2022 casts a gloomy picture of gender equality and observes that the world is not on track to achieve gender equality by 2030. The social and economic fallout from the pandemic has made the situation even bleaker. Before the pandemic, around 26 per cent of women aged 15 and older (641 million) globally have been subjected to physical and/or sexual violence by a husband or intimate partner at least once in their lifetime. During the pandemic, an intensification of violence against women were reported to have taken place. This pandemic period also dented progress in time spent on unpaid care and domestic work and also decision-making regarding sexual and reproductive health. Child marriage and female genital mutilation have also been less attended for girls and women. In 2021, nearly one in five young women were married before the age of 18 and about 200 million girls and women remained victims to FGM, mainly in specified 31 countries. Women still suffer from lack of legal right to autonomy over their own bodies. Further, despite women's leadership in responding to COVID-19, they still trail men in securing the decision-making positions. Progress in women's access to leadership positions, in both political and economic spheres, remains sluggish. As to Protection of women's land and property rights, it is still a long way to go, though positive results have been achieved in succession rights and in protection from being disposed in land transactions. The Report concludes that accelerated action is needed to expand comprehensive implementation of gender-responsive budgeting to strengthen gender equality objectives and strengthen its monitoring and evaluation.

Goal 6: Ensure Availability and Sustainable Management of Water and Sanitation for All

The drinking water services increased from its proportion of global population of 70 per cent in 2015 to 74 per cent in 2020 leaving 2 billion people still to be covered within that year. Eight out of

10 people who lack even basic drinking water service live in rural areas, and about half of them live in less developed countries. The progress of drinking water, sanitation and hygiene services is needed to be picked up speed to cover the gaps of these essential services. It is estimated that meeting drinking water, sanitation and hygiene targets by 2030 will require a fourfold increase in the pace of progress. The Report also notes rising demand for water due to rapid population growth, urbanization and increasing pressure from agriculture, industry and the energy sector. Historical misuse, poor management and the over-extraction and contamination of freshwater and groundwater supplies have exacerbated water stress and deteriorated water-related ecosystems. Additionally, the world's wetlands are being lost at an alarming rate which calls for protection and restoration of them on a massive scale. Looking at improving water quality, the Report mentioned that assessments in 2020 of rivers, lakes and aquifers in 97 countries showed that 60 per cent of water was of good ambient quality. However, of the 76, 000 water bodies assessed, only 1 per cent was in the poorest countries. For early remediation of water pollution, the Report also suggests for active monitoring with technical and financial support for such poorest countries. It concludes that for ensuring a sustainable and equitable distribution of water to meet all needs, the average global implementation rate of improved water resources management needs to double. Additional efforts are needed to increase investment in water and sanitation and to further cooperation among countries sharing trans-boundary waters.

Goal 7: Ensure Access to Affordable, Reliable, Sustainable and Modern Energy for All

The Report mentions about positive advancement towards sustainable energy targets. The global electricity access rate increased from 83 per cent in 2010 to 91 per cent in 2020. Over this period, the number of people without electricity shrank from 1.2 billion to 733 million. However, the current pace of progress is insufficient to achieve Goal 7 by 2030. Due to COVID-19, the pace of progress has slowed in recent years. During 2018-2020, the electricity access rate rose by an average of 0.5 percentage points annually compared to 0.8 percentage points in 2010-2018. As to the access to clean cooking fuels, it increased by 12 percentage points, reaching 69 per cent between 2010 and 2020 leaving 2.4 billion still dependent on polluting cooking systems. Intensified efforts are needed in least developed countries to jump-start access to clean cooking fuels and technologies. As to the climatic objective performances, the share of renewables in total final energy consumption reached 17.7 per cent in 2019, 1.6 percentage points higher than in 2010. However, total renewable energy consumption increased by a quarter over this period. As regards the climate goal of reducing greenhouse gas emissions and bridging huge disparities in access to modern sustainable energy, a major push in the deployment of renewables, with massive mobilization of finances would be needed.

Goal 8: Promote Sustained, Inclusive and Sustainable Economic Growth, Full and Productive Employment and Decent Work for All

The Goal-8 has been hit hardest by COVID-19 pandemic and reversed progress achieved earlier towards decent work for all. However, the global economy started to improve slowly. Globally, real gross domestic product (GDP) per capita increased by 1.4 per cent in 2019, then fell sharply in 2020, by 4.4 per cent, rebounding in 2021 at an estimated growth rate of 4.4 per cent. Recovery patterns however, vary perceptibly across regions, countries, sectors and labour market groups.The global real GDP per capita was projected to increase by 3.0 per cent in 2022, and 2.5 per cent in 2023 but the conflict in Ukraine is expected to seriously set back global economic growth in 2022. The COVID-19 has also adversely affected global labour productivity. In 2020, sharp declines were seen in both output and employment, and global output per worker dropped by 0.6 per cent affecting small firms and the poorest countries the most. Labour market recovery remains also shaky. The global unemployment rate is projected to remain above its 2019 level of 5.4 per cent, at least until 2023. In 2021, unemployment declined slightly to 6.2 per cent, which still translates into 28 million more unemployed persons in 2021 than in 2019. Furthermore, the level of unemployment underestimates the full employment impact of the COVID-19 crisis, since many who left the labour force have not returned. In 2019, 2 billion people worldwide (60% of global employment) worked in the informal sector. Emerging evidence from 29 countries shows that informal employment was disproportionately affected by job losses in most of these countries in 2020. The pandemic-related disruptions have also been forcing millions of children into child labour. Worldwide, 160 million children (63 million girls and 97 million boys) were engaged in child labour at the beginning of 2020. This is an increase of 8.4 million children since 2016, translating to almost 1 out of 10 children engaged in child labour worldwide. Finally, the proportion of the world's youth not engaged in either education, employment or training (NEET) increased from 21.8 per cent in 2015-2019 to 23.3 per cent in 2020, due to the pandemic. Although youth represented only 13 per cent of total employment before the crisis, they made up 34.2 per cent of the 2020 decline in employment. Youth training, education and employment have suffered massive disruptions, with women facing the biggest challenges.

Goal 9: Build Resilient Infrastructure, Promote Inclusive and Sustainable Industrialization and Foster Innovation

That resilient infrastructure and good industrial base can better cope with the adverse impact of COVID-19 is amply demonstrated. Economies with a diversified industrial sector and strong infrastructure (e.g. transport, internet connectivity and utility services) sustained less damage and are experiencing faster recovery. After dropping 1.3 per cent in 2020, global manufacturing production grew by 7.2 per cent in 2021, surpassing its pre-pandemic level. However, recovery remains uneven among countries. As a matter of record, manufacturing in more developed countries has rebounded, leaving least developed countries behind.

Jobs in manufacturing have not regained ground lost during the pandemic. Globally, the share of manufacturing jobs in total employment declined from 13.7 per cent in 2019 to 13.1 per cent in 2020. The impact has been particularly pronounced in middle-income countries. Women, youth and low- and middle-skilled workers suffered the most losses. Small-scale enterprises were hit hard by the pandemic, and many collapsed. Due to their scale, limited financial resources and greater dependency on supply chains, these industries are more vulnerable to economic downturns than their larger-scale counterparts. On the other hand, higher-technology industries have proved far more resilient in crises than their lower-tech counterparts. Overall, higher-technology industries performed better and recovered faster, providing a strong example of how important technological innovation is to achieving Goal 9.

Goal 10: Reduce Inequality within and among Countries

The gains in reduction of income inequality achieved before the COVID-19 appeared to be reversing the positive trends. Those with relatively low incomes are found at risk of falling behind. Projections have indicated that 'between-country inequality' rose by 1.2 per cent between 2017 and 2021, the first such increase in a generation. Before the pandemic, inequality was expected to have fallen by 2.6 per cent over the same period. The pandemic has also intensified structural and systemic discrimination. Emerging markets and developing economies are experiencing slow recoveries, widening disparities in income between countries. Such discrimination affected women and persons with disabilities at heightened risk. Roughly one in five persons has experienced discrimination on at least one of the grounds prohibited under international human rights law. The COVID-19 has increased relative poverty in many countries. Usually, the proportion of the population living on less than half the national median income is an important measure of social exclusion, relative poverty and inequality of income distribution within a country. Before COVID-19, 13 per cent of people, on average, lived on less than half the national median income. Recent data show that the effects of the pandemic have intensified social exclusion. Additionally, Labour income data show a decline in the labour share of income from 2014 to 2019—from 54.1 per cent to 52.6 per cent which indicates an upward pressure on inequality.The pandemic had heavy toll on migration as well. Last year, 5,895 people died fleeing their countries *via* various routes. This surpassed pre-pandemic figures and makes 2021 the deadliest year on record for migrants since 2017. The on-going war in Ukraine has created the worst refugee crisis in recent history.

Goal 11: Make Cities and Human Settlements Inclusive, Safe, Resilient and Sustainable

More than half of the world population live in the cities. About one in four urban dwellers lived in slums or informal settlements in 2020 which translate into more than 1 billion people. This is a critical mass who needs to be lifted out of poverty and live free from exclusion and inequality to achieve sustainable Development Goals. Air pollution poses a significant threat to human health and mortality worldwide. In 2019, Global $PM_{2.5}$ concentrations have steadily decreased, with an 11 per cent reduction over a decade. Despite this progress, 99 per cent of the world's urban population live in areas that exceed the new WHO guidelines on air quality, established in 2021, for $PM_{2.5}$ of less than 5 micrograms per cubic metre. People in low- and middle-income countries are disproportionately affected by outdoor air pollution, with 91 per cent of the 4.2 million premature deaths. Furthermore, only about half the world's city dwellers have convenient access to public transportation. According to 2020 data from 1, 510 cities around the world, only about 37 per cent of urban areas are served by public transport. Due to variations in population density within cities, this translates to 52 per cent of the urban population with convenient access to public transport. City governments still have a massive task ahead of them in putting in place access to safe, and reliable public transport systems. As cities continue to grow, the long standing problem of municipal solid waste continues to mount. In 2022, an average of 82 per cent of municipal solid waste globally was being collected and 55 per cent was being managed in controlled facilities. The gap between the collection rate and controlled management rate suggests open dumpsites and call for controlled management of municipal solid waste. Open public spaces in congested urban areas play a vital role in social and economic life, but are not widely accessible. Data for 2020 from 962 cities around the world point to poor distribution of such spaces. Only about 37.8 per cent of urban residential neighbourhoods are conveniently located within 400 metres walking distance to an open public space. That translates to about 45.2 per cent of the urban population. The deep inequalities exposed by the COVID-19 pandemic and other cascading crises call for initiatives to redesign and retrofit the spatial configuration of urban areas for furthering f sustainable urban development.

Goal 12: Ensure Sustainable Consumption and Production Patterns

Domestic material consumption (DMC) measures the total amount of materials directly used by an economy to meet the demands for goods and services which in turn pushes material-intensive production. Increased dependence on natural resources exacerbates the pressure on sensitive ecosystems that ultimately affects both human health and the economy. At aggregate level too much food is being lost or wasted—in every country everyday. In 2020, an estimated 13.3 per cent of the world's food was lost after harvesting and before reaching retail markets. In addition, an estimated 17 per cent of total food available to consumers (931 million metric tons) is wasted at household, food service and retail levels. Such loss or waste have substantial bearing on improving food security and decreasing the environmental footprint of food production and consumption. The vast majority of the world's electronic waste is not being safely managed. The rapid rise in this e-waste is driven by growing consumption, short product life cycles and minor repairs. In 2019, the amount of e-waste generated globally was 7.3 kilograms per capita, out of which only 1.7 kilograms was managed in an environmentally sound way and the rest pollutes the environment and negatively affects human health. Further, renewable energy is taking off in developing countries overall, but the poorest, most disadvantaged countries are lagging behind. Additionally, fossil fuel subsidies remain alarmingly high, despite a temporary drop in 2020 which also explain less than satisfactory renewable energy growth.

Goal 13: Take Urgent Action to Combat Climate Change and its Impacts

Rising global greenhouse gas emissions are resulting in record-breaking temperatures and more extreme weather. In 2020, concentrations of global greenhouse gases reached new hights, and real-time data point to continued increases. As these concentrations rise, so does the Earth's temperature. In 2021, the global mean temperature was about 1.11 ± 0.13 °C above the pre-industrial level (from 1850 to 1900), making it one of the seven warmest years on record (2015 to 2021). Fossil fuel emissions rebounded to a record hight in 2021, erasing pandemic-related declines. In 2020, social and economic disruptions caused by COVID-19 lowered energy demand around the world. But it was only a temporary reprieve. With the phasing out of COVID-related restrictions, demand for coal, oil and gas increased. Consequently, energy-related CO_2 emissions for 2021 rose by 6 per cent, reaching their highest level ever and completely wiping out the pandemic-related reduction seen in 2020. Climate financing is just a fraction of what the United Nations says is needed to avert the worst scenarios.

Goal 14: Conserve and Sustainably Use the Oceans, Seas and Marine Resources for Sustainable Development

Human activity is endangering the planet's largest ecosystem—its oceans and seas—and affecting the livelihoods of billions of people. Increasing acidification is limiting the ocean's capacity to moderate climate change. The ocean absorbs around one-quarter of the world's annual carbon dioxide (CO_2) emissions, thereby mitigating climate change and alleviating its impacts. Ocean acidification threatens organisms and ecosystem services. As acidification worsens the ocean's capacity to absorb CO_2 from the atmosphere will diminish, limiting its role in moderating climate change.

The main sources of marine pollution are land-based, leading to a seemingly unstoppable flow of litter, waste and run-off into the ocean. In 2021, a study estimated that more than 17 million metric tons of plastic entered the world's ocean, making up the bulk (85%) of marine litter. The volume of plastic pollution entering the ocean each year is expected to double or triple by 2040, threatening all marine life. The proliferation of plastic, nutrient run-off and other forms of waste is killing marine life.

Global fish stocks are under increasing threat from overfishing and from illegal, unreported and unregulated fishing. More than a-third (35.4%) of global stocks were overfished in 2019, up from 34.2 per cent in 2017. Vast areas of the ocean are under protection, but more intensive efforts are still needed. Pressure on fish stocks is lowering the contribution of sustainable fisheries to economic growth in some regions. Accelerated action is needed to support small-scale fishers, many of who livelihoods collapsed under the pandemic.

Goal 15: Protect, Restore and Promote Sustainable use of Terrestrial Ecosystems, Sustainably Manage Forests, Combat Desertification, and Halt and Reverse Land Degradation and Halt Biodiversity Loss

The world's forest area continues to shrink, mainly due to agricultural expansion. The proportion of forests fell from 31.9 per cent of total land area in 2000 to 31.2 per cent in 2020, representing a net loss of almost 100 million hectares. Agricultural expansion is driving almost 90 per cent of global deforestation. Global efforts to promote access and benefit-sharing of genetic resources has gained momentum. The Nagoya Protocol to the Convention on Biological Diversity provides a transparent legal framework for the implementation of fair and equitable sharing of benefits arising from the utilization of genetic resources. As of February 2022, 132 countries and the European Union had ratified the Protocol, and 68 countries have devised at least one legislative, administrative or policy measure to ensure its implementation. The risk of species extinction continues to rise and is highest in Asia and small island developing States. The Red List Index, which measures the overall extinction risk of species in selected taxonomic groups, reveals a deterioration of 9.2 per cent between 2000 and 2022. Nearly half of areas identified as key for global biodiversity are under protection, the mean percentage coverage of safeguarding key biodiversity areas (KBAs) by protected areas increased from over one quarter in 2000 to nearly one-half in 2021 though progress of coverage is uneven in four regions. National planning processes are increasingly reflecting the value of biodiversity. By January 2022, 37 per cent of countries assessed are on track to achieve or exceed their national targets; 58 per cent have made progress towards their targets but at an insufficient rate; and 5 per cent reported that they are making no headway or moving away from their national targets.

Goal 16: Promote Peaceful and Inclusive Societies for Sustainable Development, Provide Access to Justice for All and Build Effective, Accountable and Inclusive Institutions at All Levels

Civilians continue to bear the brunt of violent conflicts, with record numbers forcibly displaced. The United Nations recorded at least 13, 842 deaths associated with 12 of the world's deadliest armed conflicts in 2021. In May 2022, the number of people forced to flee conflict, violence, human rights violations and persecution has surpassed 100 million. An estimated 41 per cent of people forcibly displaced worldwide were children, according to 2021 data. Tracing is key to curbing illicit trade in small arms. Between 2016 and 2020, an average of 28 per cent of seized weapons were reported as successfully traced, according to data from 20 countries but it needs to be strengthened through better global cooperation. About a-third of the world's population—mostly women—say they feel unsafe walking alone in their local neighbourhoods at night. On average, about 69 per cent of the world's population report feeling safe walking alone at night in the area in which they live—a proportion that has remained stable from 2016 to 2021. Globally, almost 1 in 6 businesses face requests for bribe payments by public officials, most commonly in transactions involving electrical and water connections, construction-related permits, import licences, operating licences, and meetings with tax officials. Streamlined and transparent business processes can help curb corruption, which is found in every region.

Goal 17: Strengthen the Means of Implementation and Revitalize the Global Partnership for Sustainable Development

A stronger commitment to partnership and cooperation is needed to achieve the SDGs. Official Development Assistance (ODA) has not reached the targeted level nor private investment flows are well aligned with sustainable development. The digital divide continues to remain significant along with on-going trade tensions. To overcome such scenario, everyone will need to mobilize both existing and additional resources and developed countries will need to fulfil their official development assistance commitments. In 2021, net ODA flows amounted to $177.6 billion, an increase of 3.3 per cent in real terms from 2020, representing 0.33 per cent of donors' combined gross national income (GNI). Despite hitting a new peak, it still fell short of the 0.7 per cent target.

2

Sustainable Development Goals Scenario in India

The Sustainable Development Summit in its declaration stated that the implementation of this global agenda would be reviewed periodically at the national, regional and global level and accordingly annual global report in relation to the progress made on Goals and targets are published, a summary report of UN SDG Report 2022 being captured at Chapter-1. Similarly, NITI Aayog published three such reports on India's progress on SDGs : Baseline Report in 2018, second edition of the *Sustainable Development Goals (SDG) India Index*, in 2019 and the third edition of the *SDG India Index and Dashboard 2020-21*. Additionally, NITI Aayog also presented First and Second Voluntary National Review (VNR) at UN's High-Level Political Forum in the year 2017 and 2020 respectively. The updated sustainable development Goals could thus be seen with reference to (1) VNR 2020 and (2) SDG India Index and Dashboard 2020-21.

1. VNR 2020

The HLPF is the foremost international platform for follow-up and review of progress on the 17 Sustainable Development Goals (SDGs). India's second Voluntary National Review (VNR) styled *Decade of Action: Taking SDGs from Global to Local* was presented at the United Nations High-level Political Forum (HLPF) on Sustainable Development, 2020. In VNR 2020, India presented some of India's major progress areas on the SDGs like reducing multidimensional poverty, providing food safety, ensuring education for all, universalizing access to electricity, clean cooking fuel and sanitation, while also operationalizing the world's largest health insurance programme by covering 500 million citizens. It also mentioned the paradigm shift in terms of embodying a "whole-of-society" approach in letter and spirit and taking SDGs from Global to Local.

The highlights of the VNR, as captured by the UN, are produced hereunder:

"India, home to one-sixth of all humanity, holds the key to the success of the 2030 Agenda. India in its second VNR has made a paradigm shift to a "whole-of-society" approach with Government of India engaging sub-national and local governments, civil society organizations, local communities, people in vulnerable situations and the private sector.

India's commitment to the SDGs is reflected in its convergence with the national development agenda as reflected in the motto of *Sabka Saath Sabka Vikaas* (Collective Efforts for Inclusive Growth). Based on the evidence from the SDG India Index, which measures progress at the sub-national level, the country has developed a robust SDG localization model centred on adoption, implementation and monitoring at the State and district levels."

The following narrative further encapsulates India's progress across the SDGs.

***Sashakt Bharat—Sabal Bharat* (Empowered and Resilient India)**: India has successfully lifted more than 271 million people out of multidimensional poverty through economic growth and empowerment. Enhanced access to nutrition, child health, education, sanitation, drinking water, electricity and housing, has led to reduce inequalities especially among people in vulnerable situations.

***Swachh Bharat—Swasth Bharat* (Clean and Healthy India)**: Through a nationwide initiative triggered by the Clean India Campaign and the National Nutrition Mission, India achieved 100 per cent rural sanitation and sharp reduction in stunting and child and maternal mortality rates. Universal health coverage has been institutionalized through Ayushmaan Bharat, the world's largest health protection scheme which provides an annual cover of USD 7, 000 to 100 million families, covering nearly 500 million individuals.

India is at the forefront in the call for joint global action to address the COVID-19 pandemic. The country has extended medical assistance to several countries and has operationalized the SAARC COVID-19 Emergency Fund with an initial contribution of USD 10 million. Domestically, India's response to the COVID-19 pandemic includes an initial USD 22.5 billion economic stimulus package, comprehensive health coverage for front-line workers and direct cash transfers for the most vulnerable.

***Samagra Bharat—Saksham Bharat* (Inclusive and Entrepreneurial India):** Social inclusion is pursued through universalizing access to nutrition, health, education, social protection, and developing capabilities for entrepreneurship and employment. Financial inclusion through Jan Dhan-Aadhaar-Mobile (JAM) trinity—near universal access to bank accounts aided by the Jan Dhan Yojana (National Financial Inclusion Scheme); Aadhaar card (National unique identity number) for over 90 per cent of the population; and expansive access to mobile phones, has propelled new avenues of credit, insurance, and Direct Benefit Transfers (DBT) to the poor, including to over 200 million women, thereby accelerating their economic empowerment.

***Satat Bharat—Sanatan Bharat* (Sustainable India)**: India's climate action strategies call for clean and efficient energy systems, disaster resilient infrastructure, and planned eco-restoration. Acting on its nationally-determined contributions, India has electrified 100 per cent of its villages, reduced 38 million tonnes of CO_2 emissions annually through energy efficient appliances, provided clean cooking fuel to 80 million poor households, and set a target to install 450GW of renewable energy and restore 26 million hectares of degraded land by 2030. Globally, India stands third in renewable power, fourth in wind power, and fifth in solar power. India launched the Coalition for Disaster Resilient Infrastructure and the International Solar Alliance to leverage global partnerships for climate action and disaster resilience.

***Sampanna Bharat—Samriddh Bharat* (Prosperous and Vibrant India):** India is one of the fastest growing emerging market economies with a young population and burgeoning innovation and business ecosystem. With a GDP of USD 2.72 trillion in 2018-19, India strives to become a USD 5 trillion economy by 2025, and pursue an inclusive and sustainable growth trajectory by stimulating manufacturing, building infrastructure, spurring investments, fostering technological innovation, and boosting entrepreneurship.

In the spirit of South-South Cooperation, for realizing the 2030 Agenda, India supports developing countries through the USD 150 million India-UN Development Partnership Fund. In this spirit of regional and global partnerships, and the country's commitment to 'leave no one behind', India steps into the Decade of Action, drawing confidence from its experience in addressing challenges. Government of India will continue to work collaboratively with all domestic and global stakeholders to accelerate efforts for a sustainable planet for future generations."

India Index and Dashboard 2020-21

The third edition of the SDG India Index and Dashboard 2020-21 is the latest on progress made by States and Union Territories of India towards achieving the Sustainable Development Goals. From covering 13 Goals with 62 indicators in its first edition in 2018, the third edition covers 16 Goals on 115 quantitative indicators, with a qualitative assessment on Goal 17, thereby reflecting India's continuous efforts towards refining this important tool. The index represents the articulation of the comprehensive nature of the

Global Goals under the 2030 Agenda while being attuned to the national priorities.

The SDG India Index computes goal-wise scores on the 16 SDGs for each State and Union Territory. Overall State and UT scores are generated from goal-wise scores to measure aggregate performance of the sub-national unit based on its performance across the 16 SDGs. These scores range between 0–100, and if a State/UT achieves a score of 100, it signifies it has achieved the 2030 targets. The higher the score of a State/UT, the greater the distance to target achieved.

States and Union Territories are classified as below based on their SDG India Index score:

- Aspirant: 0–49
- Performer: 50–64
- Front-Runner: 65–99
- Achiever: 100

Overall Results and Findings

1. India's overall SDG score improved by 6 points—from 60 in 2019 to 66 in 2020-21. This positive stride towards achieving the targets is largely driven by exemplary country-wide performance in Goal 6 (Clean Water and Sanitation)

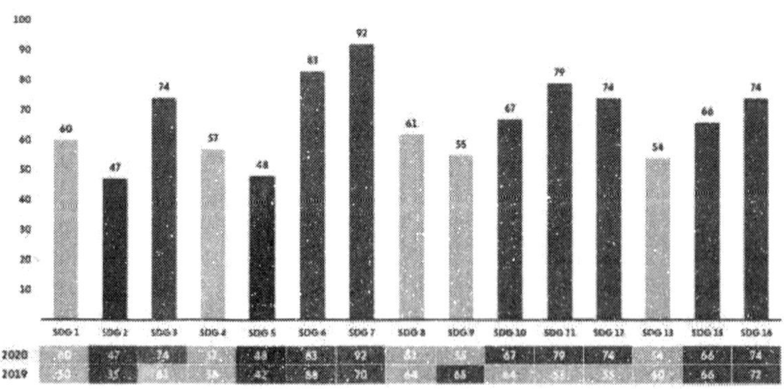

Fig. 2.1: The Report also shows the top-five and bottom-five States in SDG India

and Goal 7(Affordable and Clean Energy), where the composite Goal scores are 83 and 92, respectively. A bar-chart showing Goal-wise India results, 2019-20 and 2020-21 is captured from the India Index and Dashboard 2020-21 Report and shown below:

Table 2.1: Index 2020-21

Top 5 States	75	Kerala
	74	Himachal Pradesh, Tamil Nadu
	72	Andhra Pradesh, Goa, Karnataka, Uttarakhand
	71	Sikkim
	70	Maharashtra
Bottom 5 States	61	Chhattisgarh, Nagaland, Odisha
	60	Arunachal Pradesh, Meghalaya, Rajasthan, Uttar Pradesh
	57	Assam
	56	Jharkhand
	52	Bihar

Source: India Index and Dashboard 2020-21.

The India Index and Dashboard 2020-21 Report also captured Performance and Ranking of States and UTs on SDGs 2020-21, including change in score from last year as shown in figure 2.2:

Mizoram, Haryana, and Uttarakhand are the top gainers in 2020-21 in terms of improvement in score from 2019, with an increase of 12, 10 and 8 points, respectively.

Table 2.2: Top Fast-Moving States (Scorewise)

States	2019-20 Score	2020-21 Score	Change in Score
Mizoram	**56**	**68**	12
Haryan	**57**	**67**	10
Uttarakhand	**64**	**72**	8

Source: India Index and Dashboard 2020-21.

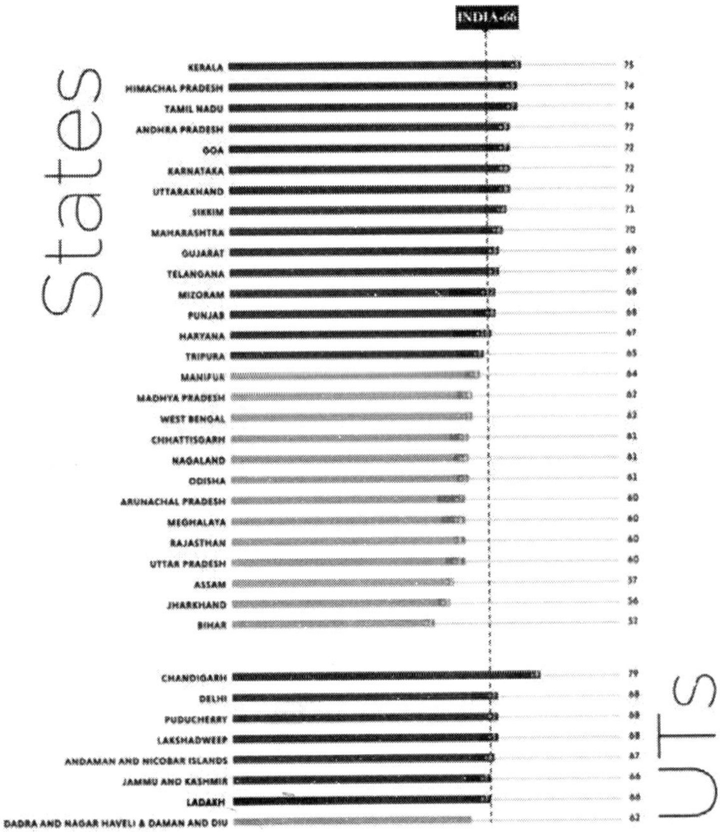

INDIA-66
States
KERALA 75
HIMACHAL PRADESH 74
TAMIL NADU 74
ANDHRA PRADESH 72
GOA 72
KARNATAKA 72
UTTARAKHAND 72
SIKKIM 71
MAHARASHTRA 70
GUJARAT 69
TELANGANA 69
MIZORAM 68
PUNJAB 68
HARYANA 67
TRIPURA 65
MANIPUR 64
MADHYA PRADESH 62
WEST BENGAL 62
CHHATTISGARH 61
NAGALAND 61
ODISHA 61
ARUNACHAL PRADESH 60
MEGHALAYA 60
RAJASTHAN 60
UTTAR PRADESH 60
ASSAM 57
JHARKHAND 56
BIHAR 52
UTs
CHANDIGARH 79
DELHI 68
PUDUCHERRY 68
LAKSHADWEEP 68
ANDAMAN AND NICOBAR ISLANDS 67
JAMMU AND KASHMIR 66
LADAKH 66
DADRA AND NAGAR HAVELI & DAMAN AND DIU 62

(*Contd.*)

Source: India Index and Dashboard 2020-21.

Fig. 2.2: The India Index and Dashboard, 2020-21 Report

While in 2019, ten States/UTs belonged to the category of Front-Runners (score in the range 65–99, including both) twelve more States/UTs find themselves in this category in 2020-21. Uttarakhand, Gujarat, Maharashtra, Mizoram, Punjab, Haryana, Tripura, Delhi, Lakshadweep, Andaman and Nicobar Islands, Jammu and Kashmir and Ladakh graduated to the category of Front-Runners (scores between 65 and 99, including both).

Table 2.3: Category of Aspirant, Performer and Front Runner

Overall	Aspirant (0-49)	Nil
	Performer (50-64)	Manipur, Madhya Pradesh, West Bengal, Chhattusgarh, Nagaland, Odisha, Arunachal Pradesh, Meghalaya, Rajasthan, Uttar Pradesh, Assam, Jharkhand, Bihar, Dadar and Nagar Haveli and Daman and Diu
	Front Runner (65-99)	Kerala, Himachal Pradesh, Tamil Nadu, Andhra Pradesh, Goa, Karnataka, Uttarakhand, Sikkim, Maharashtra, Gujarat, Telangana, Mizoram, Punjab, Haryana, Tripura, Chandigarh, Delhi, Lakshadweep, Puducherry, Andaman and Nicobar Islands, Jammu and Kashmir, Ladakh
	Achiever (100)	Nil

Source: India Index and Dashboard 2020-21.

3

Sustainable Development Goals in India and the Need for Special Focus for the Vulnerable

The updated Sustainable Development Goals reports, both at the global forum of the United Nations and those at the national monitoring forum at NITI Aayog, as discussed at Chapter-2, give a rather dismal picture on depth and breadth of performances of almost all the SDGs in India. It is worth mentioning that India's SDG ranking continues to decline. In 2022 Global Index of SDGs, the country ranked 121 out of the 163 countries. It had earlier ranked 117 in 2020 and 120 in 2021 and thus slipped for the third consecutive year. Country's preparedness in achieving the UN mandated SDGs by 2030 has worsened over the years in comparison with other countries. Needless to mention that the progress of the world to meet the SDGs largely depends on India's progress as India happens to be home to one-sixth of all humanity.

Now, as per the global report, India faces significant challenges in SDG-1 (No Poverty), Poverty headcount ratio at $1.90 a day is moderately improving and it stands at 5.9 per cent. Major challenges remain in SDG-2 (Zero Hunger), SDG-3 (Good Health and Well-Being), SDG-5 (Gender Equality). The prevalence of undernourishment (15.5%), prevalence of stunting in children under 5 years of age (34.7%), prevalence of wasting in children under 5 years of age (17.3%) are indicative of challenge ahead.

The major challenges also remain in maternal mortality rate per 100,000 live births which is still at 145, neonatal mortality rate per 1000 live births at 20.3, incidence of tuberculosis (per 100, 000 population) 188. Age-standardized death rate attributable to household, air pollution and ambient air pollution (per 100, 000 population) 184, births attended by skilled health personnel (%) 81.4, and subjective well-being (average ladder score, worst 0-10 best) 3.6. Gender Equality goal also remains a major challenge with ratio of female-to-male mean years of education received (%) 62.1, ratio of female-to-male labour force participation rate (%) 26.8, and Seats held by women in national parliament (%) 14.4. Even in clean water and sanitation goals, major challenges remains regarding population using at least basic sanitation services (%) 71.3 and anthropogenic wastewater that receives treatment (%) 2.2. As for decent work and economic growth, major challenges are Adjusted GDP growth (%) -3.6 (2020). Performance of the country is not good regarding industry, innovation and infrastructure covered under SDG-9. A big challenge remains in population using the internet (%) 43 and Expenditure on research and development (% of GDP) 0.7. The report also states that Indian cities are not even sustainable and major challenges remains in the areas like proportion of urban population living in slums (%) 34.8, annual mean concentration of particulate matter of less than 2.5 microns in diameter (PM2.5) ($\mu g/m^3$) 90.6, and access to improved water source, piped (% of urban population) 65.9.

As against this worldview of the status of SDGs implementation in India, it is worthwhile to look at the picture emerging out in the states of India as per NITI Aayog's Dashboard Report 2022. A summary of the highlights. Goal-wise is captured to indicate the status of SDGs inside the country.

Goal-1: The southern states of Kerala, Tamil Nadu, and Andhra Pradesh have had the most success in reducing poverty, with isolated triumphs in the North East and the Himalayan state of Uttarakhand. With the addition of Goa, Haryana, Himachal Pradesh, and Punjab, the aforementioned states have already met or are on their way to meeting the GOI aim of halving the national poverty rate. Andhra Pradesh, Kerala, Tamil Nadu, and Telangana are among the Indian states having the highest rates of health insurance coverage, which is crucial for avoiding poverty. Various central and northern states ranging from Bihar in the east to Maharashtra in the west, on the other hand, have struggled to reduce poverty, partly due to a lack of rural opportunities and partly due to urban influences. Nearly 40 per cent of the population of Chhattisgarh lives below the national poverty line.

Goal-2: States' SDG index scores for Goal 2 range from 19 to 80, while UTs' SDG index scores range from 27 to 97. Kerala and Chandigarh, respectively, is the best-performing state and UT. In the category of Front Runners, seven states and four UTs earned a spot (score range between 65 and 99. In the Aspirants category, however, eleven states and two UTs dropped behind (with index scores less than 50).

Goal-3: States' SDG index scores for Goal 3 range from 59 to 86, while UTs' SDG index scores range from 68 to 90. Gujarat and Delhi, respectively, are the best-performing states and UTs. In the category of Front Runners, twenty-one states and all UTs received a spot (score range between 65 and 99. No state or territory was included in the Aspirants category (with an Index score less than 50).

Goal-4: States' SDG index scores for Goal 4 range from 29 to 80, while UTs' SDG index scores range from 49 to 79. Kerala and Chandigarh, respectively, are the best-performing states and UTs. In the category of Front Runners, five states and three UTs earned a spot (score range between 65 and 99). In the Aspirants category, however, nine states and two UTs dropped behind (with Index scores less than 50).

Goal-5: States' SDG index scores for Goal 5 range from 25 to 64, whereas UTs' SDG index scores range from 33 to 68. The top performances among the States and UTs are Chhattisgarh and the Andaman & Nicobar Islands, respectively. In the category of Front Runners, no state received a spot (score range between 65 and 99).

Two UTs (Andaman and Nicobar Islands and Puducherry) qualified for the Front Runners category. In the Aspirants category, fourteen states and three UTs trailed behind (with Index scores less than 50).

Goal-6: States' SDG index scores for Goal 6 range from 54 to 100, whereas UTs' SDG index scores range from 61 to 100. With a score of 100, Goa and Lakshadweep are the highest performers among the States and UTs, respectively. In the category of Front Runners, twenty-five states and six UTs were selected. Two States and one UT belonged in the Performers category, despite the fact that no State/UT was behind in the Aspirants category.

Goal-7: For Goal 7, the SDG index score ranges from 50 to 100 for States and 71 to 100 for UTs. Fifteen states and five UTs have been placed in the Achievers category (with an Index score of 100), while twelve states and three UTs have been placed in the Front Runners category (score range between 65 and 99).

Goal-8: States' SDG index scores for Goal 8 range from 36 to 78, while UTs' SDG index scores range from 47 to 70. Himachal Pradesh and Chandigarh, respectively, are the best-performing States and UTs. In the category of Front Runners, seven states and three UTs earned a spot (score range between 65 and 99). Three states and one UT, on the other hand, trailed in the Aspirants group (with Index scores less than 50).

Goal-9: States' SDG index scores for Goal 9 range from 24 to 72, while UTs' SDG index scores range from 23 to 66. Gujarat and Delhi, respectively, are the best-performing states and UTs. Six states and one UT received a spot in the Front Runners category (score range between 65 and 99). In the Aspirants category, however, fourteen states and six UTs lagged (with Index scores less than 50).

Goal-10: States' SDG index scores for Goal 10 range from 41 to 88, while UTs' SDG index scores range from 62 to 100. Meghalaya (Achiever, with an Index score of 100) and Chandigarh (Achiever, with an Index score of 100) are the best-performing States and UTs, respectively. In the category of Front Runners, twenty states and six UTs were selected (score range between 65 and 99). Four states, on the other hand, trailed in the Aspirants group (with Index scores less than 50).

Goal-11: States' SDG index scores for Goal 11 range from 39 to 91, while UTs' SDG index scores range from 56 to 98. Punjab and Chandigarh, respectively, are the best-performing States and UTs. In the category of Front Runners, twenty-two states and five UTs were selected (score range between 65 and 99). Three states, however, trailed in the Aspirants category (with Index scores less than 50).

Goal-12: States' SDG index scores for Goal 12 range from 47 to 99, while UTs' SDG index scores range from 50 to 95. Tripura and Ladakh, as well as Jammu & Kashmir, are the best-performing among states and union territories, respectively. In the category of Front Runners, twenty-three states and five UTs were selected (score range between 65 and 99). Goa, on the other hand, lagged in the Aspirants category (with Index scores less than 50).

Goal-13: States' SDG index scores for Goal 13 range from 16 to 70, while UTs' SDG index scores range from 18 to 77. Odisha and the Andaman and Nicobar Islands, respectively, are the best-performing States and UTs. In the category of Front Runners, six states and three UTs earned a spot (score range between 65 and 99). Ten states and two UTs, on the other hand, trailed in the Aspirants group (with Index scores less than 50).

Goal-14: The nine coastal states' SDG index scores for goal 14 range from 11 to 82. Odisha and Andhra Pradesh fall into the Front Runner category (scores ranging from 65 to 99, including both), whereas Tamil Nadu is classified as an Aspirant (score less than 50). The remaining six coastal states are categorized as Performers (Score range of 50 to 64).

Goal-15: States' SDG index scores for goal 15 range from 43 to 93, while UTs' SDG index scores range from 27 to 85. Arunachal Pradesh and Chandigarh, respectively, are the best-performing States and UTs. In the category of Front Runners, thirteen states and four UTs were selected (score range between 65 and 99). Four states and one UT, on the other hand, trailed in the Aspirants group (with Index scores less than 50).

Goal-16: Through transparent and responsible institutions at all levels, India aspires to build an atmosphere of peace, justice, and good governance. India has made a number of steps to meet its goals. India's citizens are empowered by a powerful framework of rights-based legislation, The Right to Information Act, 2005.

Goal-17: The final goal is to form partnerships between governments, business organisations, non-profits, and civil society for sustainable development goals to achieve their full potential. Goal 17 establishes criteria for countries to fully mobilise domestic resources for sustainable development through more taxation and lower debt payment, while also attracting resources from abroad through improved remittance policies, increased ODA and FDI, and investment promotion regimes. On the technological front, it makes use of North-South cooperation to preferentially share the knowledge and materials that poorer countries need to get on their feet, particularly by boosting the usage of ICTs (Information and Communication Technologies) across national and international markets.

Looking ahead : Reaching the Vulnerable

The Reports on Sustainable Development Goals, both the Global and the NITI Aayog give us aggregated picture of current status of implementation of Sustainable Development Goals at different levels. It does not give us any picture of people who are vulnerable and needed to be especially empowered. The Sustainable Development Summit committed that all people must enjoy a basic standard of living through social protection systems and that children and young women and men are critical agents of change and would need to find in the new Goals a platform to channel their infinite capacities for activism into the creation of a better world. It also underscored that Sustainable Development recognizes that eradicating poverty in all its forms and dimensions, combating inequality within and among countries, preserving the planet, creating sustained, inclusive and sustainable economic growth and fostering social inclusion are linked to each other and are interdependent. Based on Universal Declaration of Human Rights, as well as other international instruments relating to human rights and international law it required promotion of human rights and fundamental freedoms without distinction of race, sex, disability or other status. The clarion call of the Summit and of the new global agenda is that "nobody should be left behind".

For transparent and visible impact of the implementation of the SDGs on the vulnerable and that nobody should be left out, it requires the implementing authorities to address the needs of the vulnerable in focused manner having regard to the plural, divergent and special nature of interventions for each of the vulnerable community in all SDGs in a country location. It is the common understanding and usual practice of any government system that a general programme of life support and incidental necessities meant for all would also be able to take care of special needs of the vulnerable. The history and development experiences suggest that the implementation of common general programme seldom reaches to the vulnerable and voiceless social group and that a dedicated Support Plan/Sub-Plan is needed to be structured for them.

Given the above background and the need to understand sustainable development needs of such vulnerable group, an attempt has been made to classify first order categories of them in India that deserves priority consideration. They belong to the category of Children, Persons with disabilities, the Women, the Aged and the Scheduled Tribes in India.

4
Prioritising Sustainable Development Goals for the Children

A child is a marvel of nature, just as the growth of a child is a natural phenomenon. A healthy child is an asset of the family and also the builder of the country for tomorrow. Accordingly, the well-beings of children are focus areas of the family and the country government at every stage of their growing up. The macro-view in the Annual report of the State of Children of the UNICEF reveals alarming gaps to the growth of child around the world. This unhappy state of affairs continues even after the path-breaking Convention of Child Rights under UNO in 1989. The children stand to sufferer in various parts of the world on counts of hunger, child health, primary education, discrimination, violence and the like.

The Human Development Report also captures the state of children of a country in a roundabout way through HDI which is a summary measure of average achievements of three basic dimensions of human development, namely a long and healthy life, a decent standard of living and access to knowledge. A long and healthy life is measured by life expectancy. Knowledge level is measured by mean years of schooling. As per the Human Development Report 2005, India ranked 127 out of 177 countries, 119th rank out of 169 countries in Human Development Report 2010 and 130th position among the 188 countries in the 2015 Human Development Report.

The 2020 Human Development Report presents the 2019 HDI (values and ranks) for 189 countries, India's HDI value for 2019 being 0.645—which put the country in the medium human development category—positioning it at 131 out of 189 countries. This position is rather embarrassing for a major developing country like India and needs serious introspection.

The unhappy state of the status of the children in India needs to be examined more deeply with reference to the Child Development Index (CDI). The CDI was started in 2008 as a complement to the UNDP's HDI to keep a tab on the progress on Child's well-being. The CDI is an index of combined performance measures specific to children—education, health and nutrition/Index scores reflect the average level of performance across a set of eight indicators related to child health, education, labour, marriage, childbirth and violence—to produce a score on a scale 0 to 100. A zero score would be best score. The higher the score, the worse the children are faring. As per the Child Development Index (CDI), India ranked 100th out of 141 countries in 2005-2010.The End of Childhood Index published by the Global Child Report, 2020 put India at the rank of 115 with score 784 signalling an unhappy growing up of children in India.

The UN Sustainable Development Goals (SDGs) adopted on 25th September, 2015 aimed to end hunger, assure gender equity, and build a life of dignity for all over the world. It gave a clarion call of a new framework of "Transforming Our World: the 2030 Agenda for Sustainable Development". Among the 17 goals to this agenda, focus was on complete poverty eradication, zero hunger, quality education, gender equality, children well-being, sustainable cities and communities and clean water and sanitation. Since the SDGs are universal in nature, it did not earmark a separate goal for the children but interwoven them within the general goals and stipulated that by the year 2030, all children will have equitable access to quality early childhood development and early learning opportunities and no one will be left behind. The 2030 Agenda of Sustainable Development Goals enjoins a commitment of the country governments to realizing children components as those have been designed on consideration of the Convention of the Rights of the Child. It would be worth while to focus on broad areas where children have to be taken care of.

Global Status of the Children in Brief

The UNICEF in its the State of the World's Children 2021 mentions that the COVID-19 pandemic had adversely affected the mental health of a generation of children. In its earlier Report on the State of the World's Children 2020 also, it highlighted the adverse effect during pandemic and noted that School closures, increased vulnerability to abuse, mental health strains and loss of access to vital services had hurt the children deeply around the world.However, the effects were not uniform but varied which accentuated the inequality divide, and the poorest countries and disadvantaged communities suffered most. Before the pandemic, the 2019 edition of *The State of the World's Children* took an overview of the progress in the past two decades and observed that despite perceptible progress, one-third of children under age 5 are malnourished—stunted, wasted or overweight—while two-thirds are at risk of malnutrition and hidden hunger owing to poor quality of their diets. It also noted that the broken food system is responsible for the children not to get the diets they need to grow healthy. For removing malnutrition, it underscores the need to put children's rights at the heart of food systems.

Status of Children in India in Brief

The macro-view of state of the child in India portrayed by UNICEF, gives a picture of high concern. It speaks of absence quality of life of the children with high level of malnutrition (38.4% of children are stunted), poor learning outcomes (only 42.5 per cent of children in grade three can read a grade one text), vaccine preventable diseases and child labour.

Despite having adverse sex ratio of 900 girls for every 1000 boys, more girls die than boys. Globally 7 per cent more boys die under the age of 5 compared to girls, but in India, 11 per cent more girls die under the age of 5.

Children staying in rural areas, slums and urban poor families and those belonging to Scheduled Castes, tribal communities and other disadvantaged populations suffer from multiple deprivations related to poverty, malnutrition, access to quality health services, child marriage, poor school attendance, low learning outcomes, lack of sanitation facilities, hygiene, and access to improved water.

The huge sizes of adolescent population of 253 million are especially vulnerable to poor nutritional status. More than half (54%) of adolescent girls have anaemia compared to 30 per cent of boys, and have low Body Mass Index. Added to them is challenges of child marriage and adolescent pregnancies which have an intergenerational impact and affecting their ability to live empowered. India is home to the largest number of child brides in the world.

India has also one of the highest rates of violence against women and between 60-90 per cent of girls face sexual harassment/ violence in public spaces. India is also highly prone to disasters including flooding, droughts, earthquakes, refugee flows and climate change that all impact on the life of the children.

Research Questions

The question that springs up is why the status of the children in India is rather on the lower side *vis-à-vis* the children of the world or on the performances of SDGs related indicators. There could be many plausible reasons. Let us probe them under three framework of queries for probable answers.

A. Is it because that child development initiative in India is not Right-based?
B. Is it because that child development initiative in India are not adequately or comprehensively addressed or budgeted?
C. Is it because those child development initiatives in India are not properly supervised and monitored?

Let us probe all of them individually and sequentially.

A. Is it because that child development initiative in India is not Right-based?

Child Rights and the Sustainable Development Goals in India

The Sustainable Development Summit envisaged a world free of poverty, hunger, disease and want, where all life can thrive. It also envisaged a world free of fear and violence and also a world with universal literacy. People who are vulnerable must be empowered and the needs of the children met for fulfilment of all aspects leading to the complete growth of a child. This approach of SDGs was also built upon the Conventions of Child Rights, 1989. The approach of the Sustainable Development Goals needs to have one to one correspondence with the governance culture of the implementing country for obtaining desired outcome on the children. In India, child rights have been designed to be protected under three different forums: (a) Constitution of India, (b) A host of legislations, and (c) Indian Penal Code. Incidentally, all of them were in place before the coming of the Sustainable Development Goals.

(a) Constitution of India

The Constitution of India in its Part III (Fundamental Rights) and Part IV (Directive Principles of State Policy) guarantees under the articles mentioned below, rights to the children of India which have bearing with different SDGs as indicated in brackets:

PART III (Fundamental Rights)

Article 14: Citizens of India, including children, must be treated equally before law and must be given equal protection by the law without any discrimination or arbitrariness (Linked to SDG -16.3).

Article 15(3): Discrimination is prohibited by the Constitution. However, it shall not hold a ground to prevent the state from making special provisions for women and children for their benefit (Linked to SDG-16.3).

Article 21: No person shall be deprived of his life or personal liberty without due process of law. A person has the right to adequate food, shelter, clothing etc. Such life shall not mean mere animal existence (Linked to SDG-16.3).

Article 21A: The State shall provide free and compulsory education to all the children falling in the age group of six to fourteen years in such manner as the State may, by law, determine (Linked to SDG-4.1, 4.2, & 4.3).

Article 23: Prohibits trafficking in human beings and beggar or any other form of forced labour (Linked to SDG-9.7).

Article 24: Prohibits employment of children under the age of fourteen years in a factory, mine or in any other hazardous employment (Linked to SDG-8.7).

PART IV (Directive Principles of State Policy)

Article 39(e): The state shall thrive to ensure that the tender age of children is not abused and that citizens are not forced by economic necessity to enter avocations unsuited to their age or strength (Linked to SDG-8.7).

Article 39(f): The state shall ensure children are given opportunities and facilities to develop in a healthy manner and in conditions of freedom and dignity. It must also be ensured that childhood and youth are protected against exploitation and against moral and material abandonment (Linked to SDG-8.7).

Article 41: The state is obliged to, within its economic capacity and development, secure provisions for educational opportunities and facilities (Linked to SDG-4.4, 4.5, & 4.7).

Article 44: The state shall make all possible efforts to secure a Uniform Civil Code for all the citizens, thereby implying a uniform code for the adoption of children (Linked to SDG-16.3).

Article 45: The state shall endeavour to provide free and compulsory education to children until they attain the age of fourteen years (Linked to SDG-4.1).

Article 46: It is the duty of the state to promote the educational and economic interests of weaker sections of the society with special care and therefore, the children therein (Linked to SDG-4.4).

Article 47: The state is duty-bound to raise the level of nutrition and the standard of living and to improve public health, including that of children (Linked to SDG-2.1, & 2.2).

Article 51(c): International laws and treaties shall be respected by the state to every possible extent, including the CRC and its optional protocols, Optional Protocol to CRC on Sale of Children, Child Prostitution and Child Pornography and Optional Protocol to CRC on the Involvement of Children in Armed Conflict (Linked to SDG-8.7, 17.9, 17.2, 17.14, 17.15, & 17.16).

Article 51-A(k): It shall be the duty of every citizen of India who is a parent or guardian to provide opportunities for education to his child or, as the case may be, ward between the age of six and fourteen years (Linked to SDG-4.1).

(b) A Host of Legislations

Apart from constitutional provisions, a variety of legislations have been passed in the country for the growth, development and protection of the child. Such legislations do address and impact promotional and regulatory areas of SDGs as mentioned hereunder:

1. **Hindu Adoption and Maintenance Act, 1956:** The Act was enacted to govern laws relating to adoption of children and maintenance (Linked to SDG-1.3).
2. **Guardians and Wards Act, 1890:** The Act supersedes all the laws regarding guardianship of a child. It is a universal code specifically designed for Muslims, Parsis, Christians and Jews as their personal laws do not allow full adoption but only guardianship (Linked to SDG-10.4).
3. **The Children Act, 1960:** The Act provides for the care, protection, maintenance, welfare, training, education and rehabilitation of neglected or delinquent children and for the trial of delinquent children (Linked to SDG 1.3, & 5.2).

4. **The Women's and Children's (Licensing) Act, 1956:** The Act was enacted with an object to protect women and children from exploitation and inhuman activities going on in institutions. It mandates the institutions for women and children to get a licence from the licensing authority before establishing or maintaining the institution (Linked to SDG-1.3, & 5.2).
5. **Orphanages and Other Charitable Homes (Supervision and Control) Act, 1960:** The Act provides for the supervision and control of orphanages, homes for neglected women or children and other like institutions (Linked to SDG 1.3, & 5.2).
6. **Juvenile Justice (Care and Protection of Children) Act, 2000:** This Act is one of the important Acts in India for the children in need of care and protection and also children in conflict with the law. It requires that the state provides free legal support to the juveniles, and proper care and protection is provided to those in need. It also calls for a child-friendly approach in adjudication and disposition of matters involving children (Linked to SDG-1.3, & 5.2).
7. **The Protection of Children from Sexual Offences Act, 2012:** The Act aims at punishing the offenders who are guilty of sexual offences against children below the age of 18 years of age. It also lays down procedures for the trial, such as, the name of child victim shall not be disclosed, proceedings of the case are to be conducted in court with cameras recording the trial, accused is not to be kept in-front of the child victim during examination or cross-examination etc. (Linked to SDG-5.2, & 16.2).
8. **Immoral Traffic (Prevention) Act (Amended in 1986), 1956:** This Act with respect to children deals with person(s) who procure or attempt to procure any child for prostitution or person(s) who are found with a child in a brothel (it is presumed child has been detained for the purpose of prostitution) and punishes them. It also provides for the due care of rescued children (Linked to SDG-5.2).

9. **Probation of Offenders Act, 1958:** This Act with the help of the Juvenile Justice Act, 2000 tries to ensure that no person under the age of 21 years faces imprisonment (Linked to SDG-1.3, & 5.2).
10. **The Pre-Natal Diagnostic Techniques (Regulation and Prevention of Misuse) Amendment Act, 2000:** The main objective of the Act is to regulate and prevent the pre-natal sex determination in order to prevent female foeticide (Linked to SDG-1.3, & 5.2).
11. **Infant Milk Substitutes, Feeding Bottles and Infant Foods (Regulation of Production, Supply and Distribution) Act, 1992:** The Act aims at the protection and promotion of breast-feeding and ensuring regulation of proper use of infant foods and matters incidental thereto (Linked to SDG-5.3).
12. **The Prohibition of Child Marriage Act, 2006:** The Act defines child marriage as marriage in which either the girl or the boy is under age, i.e the girl is under 18 years of age or the boy is younger than 21 years (Linked to SDG-5.3).
13. **The Right of Children to Free and Compulsory Education Act, 2009:** The Act governs the modalities of the free and compulsory education for children between the age of 6 to 14 in India as required under Article 21A of the Constitution of India (Linked to SDG-4.1).
14. **The Person with Disabilities Act, 2016:** The Act was enacted to fulfil the obligations to the UN Convention on the Right of Persons with Disabilities, which India ratified in 2007 (Linked to SDG-1.3, & 10.2).
15. **The Factories Act, 1948 (Amended in 1949, 1950, 1954 and 1987):** The Act, where adult means a person who has completed 15 year of age, serves to consolidate the law regarding labour laws and assist in formulating national policies in India with respect to occupational safety and health in factories and docks in India (Linked to SDG-5.1 5c, & 8.8).

16. **Bonded Labour System (Abolition) Act, 1976:** The Act aims at eradicating the bonded labour system in India which exploits the weaker sections of society, especially children (Linked to SDG 5.1, 5c, & 8.8).
17. **Child Labour (Prohibition and Regulation) Act, 1986:** This Act regulates the working conditions for children in employment and prohibits working of children in certain kinds of employments (Linked to SDG 5.1, 5c, & 8.8).
18. **The Commission for Protection of Child Rights (CPCR) Act, 2005:** The National Commission for Protection of Child Rights (NCPCR) is a body that works towards achieving a child right in all laws, programmes and policies and administrative mechanisms in India (Linked to SDG-5.3).

(c) Indian Penal Code (IPC)

The Indian Penal Code, 1860 on its various sections specifically protects children and their rights. Some of these sections are:

(a) **S.83:** Nothing is an offence which is done by a child above seven years of age and under twelve, who has not attained sufficient maturity of understanding to judge the nature and consequences of his conduct on that occasion (Linked to SDG-1.3).

(b) **S.292 & 293:** Selling, distribution, publishing, public exhibition or circulation of obscene material such as books, magazines, drawings, paintings etc. is prohibited under Section 292. Whoever sells, lets to hire, distributes, exhibits or circulates to any person under the age of twenty years any such obscene object as is referred to in Section 292, or offers or attempts so to do, shall be punished more severely (Linked to SDG-1.5).

(c) **S.305:** Abetment of the commission of suicide of a person below the age of 18 years is punishable under this section (Linked to SDG-5.2, & 16.2).

(d) **S.317:** Abandonment or exposure of a child for the purpose of abandonment by any of the parents or a person having the care of such child is a punishable offence (Linked to SDG-5.2, & 16.2).

(e) **S.361:** This section deals with punishing offenders who kidnap a child (male if below 16 years of age and female if below 18 years of age) (Linked to SDG-5.2, & 16.2).

(f) **S.363A:** Kidnapping or maiming children for the purpose of begging has been stated to be a punishable offence under this section (Linked to SDG-5.2, & 16.2).

(g) **S.366A:** Inducing of a minor girl under the age of 18 years to do any act that may force or seduce her to illicit intercourse with another person is punishable under S.366A (Linked to SDG-5.2, & 16.2).

(h) **S.366B:** It is an punishable offence to import a girl under 21 years of age into India from a country outside India or from Jammu and Kashmir intending that she may be forced or seduced to illicit intercourse with another person (Linked to SDG-5.2, & 16.2).

(i) **S.369:** Kidnapping a child under the age of 10 years with the intention to steal from such child is an offence (Linked to SDG-5.2, & 16.2).

(j) **S.372 & 373:** Selling, buying or hiring a person under 18 years of age for the purpose of prostitution or illicit intercourse with any person, or for any unlawful or immoral purpose is a punishable offence (Linked to SDG-5.2, & 16.2).

(k) **S.375:** A man is said to commit "rape" if has sexual intercourse with a woman with or without her consent when she is under the age of 16 years (Linked to SDG 5.2, & 16.2).

(l) **S.376:** The section provides for stringent punishments if:

1. rape is committed by management or staff of Remand Home or any other place of custody established by law or children's institution,
2. rape is committed upon a woman under 12 years of age, and
3. Gang rape is committed (Linked to SDG -5.2, & 16.2).

(m) **S.376C:** When the Superintendent or manager of a remand home or any other place of custody established under law of 'children's institution' induces or seduces a woman into sexual intercourse by taking advantage of his official position, he is entitled to stringent punishment under this section (Linked to SDG-5.2, & 16.2).

In other words, the Constitution of India, different legislations and Indian Penal Code do provide protective cover and direction for child development which are mandatory in nature. Such provisions serve also as regulatory mechanism to ensure aspects of sustainable development goals. Furthermore, such Rights of the Child focus are also discernible in the policy approach of the government as mentioned hereinunder:

Policy of the Government of India related to the Child

1. **National Policy for Children, 1974:** It is the first written policy for the children in India. It aims at providing better enforcement of constitutional rights of the children along with those granted by the CRC. Some of the provisions include free education, comprehensive health and nutritious plans etc.
2. **National Policy on Education, 1986:** The policy is extensive in nature and elementary, university and adult level education, all fall under its scope. It tries to remove inequality by making special provisions for women and other weaker sections of society such as Schedule Castes, Schedule Tribes etc.
3. **National Policy on Child Labour, 1987:** The policy endeavours to eradicate child labour from Indian society wherever necessary.
4. **National Nutrition Policy, 1993:** The National Nutrition Policy was introduced in 1993 to combat the problem of under-nutrition. It aims to address the problems by utilizing direct (short term) and indirect (long term) interventions.

5. **National Health Policy, 2002:** This is the second National Health Policy, after the first in 1983. The policy provides for Universal Immunization Programmes, health care related education in schools and free regular health check ups at schools etc.
6. **National Charter for Children, 2003**: The Government of India adopted the National Charter for Children to reiterate its commitment to the cause of children in order to see that no child remains hungry, illiterate or sick.
7. **National Plan of Action, 2005:** The National Plan of Action, 2005 details situation of child health, maternal health, nutrition, education, water and sanitation, girl child, adolescent girls and also for children in difficult circumstances.
8. **The National Policy for Children, 2013:** The National Policy for Children aims to protect and encourage the rights of thc child to survive, health, nutrition, education, development, protection, advocacy and partnership, coordination, action and monitoring, resource allocation etc.

B. Is it because that child development initiative in India are not adequately or comprehensively addressed or budgeted?

The state of children in India, far from being ideal and satisfactory as per national and international reports, needs to be examined with reference to facts as to whether child development related programmes in India are adequately and comprehensively addressed and whether required fund were budgeted for.

NITI Aayog is the nodal authority for the SDGs related activities in India. It has mapped out Goal-wise SDG related programme interventions in India across the States and Union Territories. However, the mapping does not indicate child-specific programmes under eight goals, most crucial for the children, namely,

- Child Poverty (covered under SDG-1).
- Child Nutrition (covered under SDG-2).

- Child Health (covered under SDG-3).
- Child Education (covered under SDG-4).
- Girls child and gender equality (SDG-5).
- Child sanitation and hygiene (SDG-6).
- Child-friendly safe environment (covered under SDG-11, & SDG-13).
- Child security against violence, exploitation and abuse (SDG-16).

The mapping of schemes as such does not have specific linkage meant for the children. Besides, schemes are general in nature meant for all, the children being incidental beneficiaries. As a result, schemes not having children as their centrist focus and not having consideration of their life cycle needs, lose the strength and vitality of effective intervention. A plethora of schemes is not substituted for a number of dedicated schemes compatible for implementation, monitoring and outcome of child development. In the given context, it is hardly possible to curve out exclusive list of child-specific SDGs schemes in India.

Linked with the child-specific schemes is also the concept of budgeting for them. A scheme gets its life-strength as soon as the money is budgeted for it. The budget provision is also statement of support of the government. From a budget provision of general nature of scheme, it is difficult to find out fund flow for the children as it is impossible to have actual data of coverage of targeted children. As a matter of fact, development experiences over the years has shown that that the implementation of common general programme seldom reaches to the vulnerable and voiceless social group and that dedicated schemes are needed to be structured for them. Incidentally, child budgeting, as introduced in India since 2008-09, to showcasing child related budgeted schemes in one place, is in fact a mechanistic exercise and has no linkage whatsoever with Child Plan, not to speak of addressing child components under the SDGs. Based on the rights of the child, a Sub-plan for *all* the Children needs to take care of poverty of related children, Nutrition, Health coverage, Education, Gender equality, and violence against children etc. with an eye to SDGs indicators and then budget for them.

C. Is it because those child development initiatives in India are not properly supervised and monitored?

The text book format for monitoring and supervision starts with sanction of schemes and followed by distinctive process of supervision on "Inputs-Activities-Output-Outcome –Impact". The correct behaviour of these fundamentals are the keys to ensure the ends of programme intervention. This basic mechanism is applicable equally for regulatory and promotional schemes/programmes on Child components under SDGs. Any non-structured format of monitoring does not reveal flow character of functional behaviour of programme and of its underneath grey areas. In absence of dedicated monitoring efforts, on plethora of schemes in place, it is difficult to capture the actual state of affairs, on regular basis, on protection of child rights in areas of prevention of abuse, exploitation, violence, trafficking etc. despite having substantial statutory, legislative and constitutional directions and coverage.

The existing system of supervision and monitoring in the country follows the Constitutional division of power in the Union List, Concurrent List and State List and thereafter in the linked responsibilities among the ministries of the Central Government or among the departments of the State Governments as per the related Rules of business. After the 73rd and 74th Amendments of the Constitution, the Panchayats at the appropriate tiers in the rural areas and respective Municipalities in the urban areas are also empowered to perform devolved responsibilities. Constitutionally therefore, all of these organs have responsibilities to supervise and monitor on SDGs related schemes, including its child components.

The moot question that comes up is how these decentralized federal units performed supervision and monitoring for their respective sustainable development responsibility. Unfortunately, there is no data in the public domain on such responsibilities either on Sustainable Development Goals or on related programme, and of its monitoring indicators. In fact, apart from general nature of aggregated picture state-wise, nothing seems to be available on extent of surveyed deficit, its updated coverage and the volume of gaps that are to be covered during the remaining life years of SDGs or of its annual phasing. There is a strong case of more focused supervision on SDGs including its child component at the decentralized federal units level.

Given this framework of monitoring and its limitations, it would be worthwhile to examine the effectiveness of supervision and monitoring from another way, i.e. by looking at institutions supposed to do monitoring from institutional angle, (a) on regulatory and (b) promotional areas:

(a) Regulatory

National Commission for Protection of Child Rights (NCPCR), set up by the NCPCR Act, 2005 and functional since 5th March, 2007, is the nodal authority in the country for the Child Rights with wide ranging 19 items of power for the protection of child rights, including its authority to its assessing, inquiring, examining reviewing and recommending measures for their effective implementation. Under Right to Education Act, 2009, NCPCR is also empowered to inquire into complaints relating to child's right to free and compulsory education. It also monitors the implementation of Protection of Children from Sexual Offences (POCSO) Act, 2012.

The Annual Reports of the NCPCR, while covering periodical works done in some important areas of the child rights area like juvenile Justice etc. do not convey any aggregate picture of all components of child right in India. Partners like State Commission for protection of Child Rights (SCPCR), the judiciary and police administration and others of the state government do work for protection of Child Rights in the areas of criminal justice and in furtherance of legal protection in their own routine way. The need for reforms for improved functional synergy in between the nodal departments of the state government for prevention of child labour, underage marriage and the abuse and violence of the children is real. The scope for intensive supervision of implementing and nodal functionaries is equally paramount. It is equally important to have periodical status covering all aspects of child rights in the country in wholesome manner. Incidentally, the NCPCR Act came into being a decade earlier than the Sustainable Development Summit Declaration of September 2015 and therefore, the said Act is needed to be further improved upon in the regulatory area with the new world vision of sustainable development goals.

(b) Promotional

NITI Aayog was formed through a resolution of the Union Cabinet on First January, 2015 to work as a policy think tank of the Government of India for providing directional and policy inputs. It is also the nodal authority in the country for overseeing the implementation of the 2030 agenda of sustainable development goals. It is true that though India's federal system ordains that States and Union Territories (UTs) are primarily responsible for implementation of SDGs, NITI Aayog contributed significantly to the pursuit of SDGs by sensitising different stakeholders, conducting a series of National and Regional Consultations in collaboration with UN and other partner organizations, mapping out SDGs and related targets on Central Ministries, Centrally Sponsored/Central Sector Schemes and other government initiatives, regularly reviewing progress, providing need-based technical support, facilitating mutual learning among States/UTs and ranking the performance of States/UTs on SDGs on a set of select indicators. It has played a critical role in bringing together diverse stakeholders and setting off collaboration among them for specific objectives.

NITI Aayog does not, however, have any authority either on physical supervision of the schemes taken upon under central sector/centrally sponsored or state sector schemes or of its monitoring which lies squarely with the concerned nodal ministry of the Central Government or with the departments of the State

Governments. Since most of the schemes, mapped up under SDGs, fall under the category of continuing schemes, such schemes do address other objectives of the nodal ministry/department along with sustainable development goals. Assessment of outcome of such schemes, central and state, either jointly or severally, in a given area in the context of a SDG is well-nigh impossible. This reinforces the idea that stand-alone schemes for a particular SDG are better positioned to register output and outcome through a process of supervision and monitoring and bridge the development deficit of a given area. The visibility of monitoring of outcome of schemes of the Panchayat or the Municipalities, taken up under child-specific SDGs, has also important bearing to overall impact on the SDGs.

Concluding Observations

On perusal of our research questions and to its related findings, it is observed that India did not initiate a proactive child right-based approach for the sustainable development goals for the children despite having a framework of child rights prior to the coming of the sustainable development goals. However, such constitutional perspective remotely and indirectly played its role in the sensitization of child rights under SDGs without playing very meaningful and focused role in addressing SDGs. It is also found that since mapped out schemes of SDG are general in nature, and not child centrist, and that child budget is not in place to address deficit in the indicators of child development, there is the need for proactive intervention on child focused SDGs, its budgeting and of its supervision and monitoring. Finally, SDGs *per se* are inter-connected and the intervening programmes have built-in propensity to impact compatible programme of associated goals. In that sense, there is a good scope for natural convergence among child-friendly programmes of related other goals for focused output at a possible incremental scale. Moreover, there is a need for convergence among Central Government schemes on child development; among child development schemes, both regulatory and promotional, under State Government; between the Central Government child development schemes and the State Government child development schemes; among the child development schemes of the three-tier of the Panchayats; among child development schemes of the Municipalities, and the like. A convergence framework need to be worked out for child development and put in place.

5
Refocusing the Approach towards Persons with Disabilities

The Sustainable Development Summit in its Declaration on September, 2015 gave a call to reorder the agenda of plan of action for member countries with a firm commitment that nobody should be left behind. In this transformational vision and journey, it envisaged a world of universal respect of human rights and human dignity, the rule of law, justice, equality and non-discrimination of respect for all and that equal opportunity for realizing of human potentiality should be given to all and that people who are vulnerable must be empowered. The declaration specifically mentioned persons with disabilities of whom more than 80 per cent live in poverty. It also underscored to providing inclusive and equitable quality of education at all levels—early childhood, primary, secondary, tertiary, technical and vocational training to persons with disabilities. In consideration of concern for this most vulnerable segment of population, appropriate indicators have been built in the monitoring system in the related SDGs to ensure that they are accorded due importance to outreach and outcome.

The United Nations published the first-ever UN flagship report on disability and the Sustainable Development Goals in 2018—the Disability and Development Report on the "Realization of the Sustainable Development Goals by, for and with persons with disabilities". The report demonstrates that persons with disabilities are at a disadvantage regarding most Sustainable Development Goals. Concrete action is needed to include the world's one billion persons with disabilities as both agents and beneficiaries of development. The Report calls for urgent actions to be taken for the achievement of the Sustainable Development Goals by, for and with persons with disabilities by 2030.

Subsequent to the publication of UN flagship Report on the "Realization of the Sustainable Development Goals by, for and with persons with disabilities", the UN General Assembly in December 2019, adopted two resolutions. The first resolution titled "Promoting social integration through social inclusion" (A/C.3/74/L.17/Rev.1) and the second titled "Implementation of the Convention on the Rights of Persons with Disabilities and the Optional Protocol there to: accessibility" (A/C.3/74/L.32/Rev.1) note the importance of this report for the continuing work to advance the rights of persons with disabilities in the implementation, monitoring and evaluation of the Sustainable Development Goals.

The Case of Persons with Disabilities in India—A Brief Profile

According to Census 2011 of India, out of the 121 crore population, about 2.68 crore persons are 'Persons with Disabilities' which constitutes 2.21 per cent of the total population. In an era of addressing the sustainable development goals with the agenda that "No one should be left behind" and also Government's call for 'inclusive development', focused initiatives are essential for the welfare of *Persons with Disabilities*. This calls for to have detailed picture of the persons with disability and the necessity for strengthening disability statistics in the country. A brief profile of *Persons with Disabilities in India as per census 2011* is presented in Table 5.1 and Table 5.2.

Table 5.1: Persons with Disabilitiesby Sex and Residence, India, 2011

Disabled Population by Sex and Residence, India, 2011			
Residence	**Persons**	**Males**	**Females**
Total	26810557	14986202	11824355
Rural	18631921	10408168	8223753
Urban	8178636	4578034	3600602

Source: Census of India website (http://censusindia.gov.in/ downloaded on 10.10.2019)

Table 5.2: Persons with Disabilities in India by type of Disability

Persons with Disabilities by type of Disability			
Type of Disability	**Persons**	**Male**	**Female**
Total	26810567	14986202	11824355
In seeing	5032463	2638516	2393947
In hearing	5071007	2677544	2393463
In speech	1998535	1122896	875639
In movement	5436604	3370374	2066230
Mental Retardation	1505624	870098	634916
Mental Illness	722826	415732	307094
Any other	4927011	2727828	2199183
Multiple Disability	2116487	1162604	953883

Source: Census of India website (http://censusindia.gov.in/downloaded on 10.10.2019)

The decadal change in population gives us overtime data to understand also the enormity of changing character of the persons with disability situation and locate the areas that need to be addressed as can be seen at Table 5.3.

Table 5.3: Decadal Changes of Persons with Disabilities by Sex and Residence in India

Decadal change in Disabled Population by Sex and Residence, India, 2001-2011						
Residence	**Absolute Increase**			**Percentage Decadal Growth**		
	Persons	**Males**	**Females**	**Persons**	**Males**	**Females**
Total	4903788	2380567	2523221	22.4	18.9	27.1
Rural	2243539	997983	1245556	13.7	10.6	17.8
Urban	2660249	1382584	1277665	48.2	43.3	55

Source : Census India website (http://censusindia.gov.in/ downloaded on 10.10.2019)

The state-wise position of *Persons with Disabilities* has also been captured at Table 5.4 to have an idea of enormity of size of this segment of population and the need to have dedicated efforts and distinct programme intervention to mainstream them as agents and beneficiaries of the new agenda of sustainable development goals in the different states of India.

Table 5.4: Persons with Disabilities in the States of India

State	Total Persons with Disabilities as per Census 2011
Andhra Pradesh	2266607
Arunachal Pradesh	26734
Assam	480065
Bihar	2331009
Chhattisgarh	624937
Delhi	234882
Goa	33012
Gujarat	1092302
Haryana	546374
Himachal Pradesh	155316
Jammu & Kashmir	361153
Jharkhand	769980
Karnataka	1324205

(*Contd.*)

State	Total Persons with Disabilities as per Census 2011
Kerala	761843
Madhya Pradesh	1551931
Maharashtra	2963392
Manipur	54110
Mizoram	15160
Meghalaya	44317
Nagaland	29631
Odisha	1244402
Punjab	654063
Rajasthan	1563694
Sikkim	18187
Tamil Nadu	1179963
Tripura	64346
Uttar Pradesh	4157514
Uttarakhand	185272
West Bengal	2017406
A&N Islands	6660
Chandigarh	14796
Daman & Diu	2196
D & N Haveli	3294
Lakshadweep	1615
Puducherry	30189
Total	**26810557**

Table 5.4 also shows that the five states which have maximum number of disabled population are Uttar Pradesh, Maharashtra, Bihar, Andhra Pradesh and West Bengal.

For understanding the long term quality living of the persons with disability, education and skill development are of paramount importance. Education leads to upliftment of personality and mental strength through knowledge empowerment while skill development promotes a better living for future. As a matter of fact,

Table 5.5: Schooling Status with for Persons with Disabilities in India

Total disabled population (5-19 years)			**Attending educational institution**			**Not Attending educational institution**					
						Attended educational institution earlier			**Never attended educational institution**		
Persons	**Males**	**Females**	**Persons**	**Males**	**Females**	**Persons**	**Males**	**Females**	**Persons**	**Males**	**Females**
6572999	3692554	2880445	4021301	2280040	1741261	797961	455491	342470	1753737	957023	796714

Source: www.indiastat.com downloaded on 7.9.2019.

obtaining quality education is the foundation to improving people's lives and also in a way to all goals of sustainable development. Therefore, data on *Persons with Disabilities* with a comparative picture of the attending school *vis-à-vis* those not attending schools and/or drop-outs give an indication where special schooling is essential for the betterment of this segment of people. At Table 5.5, it is attempted to capture them.

The persons with disabilities, distinguished by its plural and distinct physical or intellectual infirmities are not homogeneous. They have their own infirmities which are unique to a particular segment of this population. A fit-to-cover all *Persons with Disabilities under one* approach is not applicable for them. Therefore, multiple approaches for addressing these different categories of disabilities with different modes and methods of learning are needed which by themselves are very challenging. The policy and programme interventions in this special area have thus to be varied and distinct to address specific infirmities of individuals to ensure that nobody should be left behind for coverage, effective outreach and outcome within the overarching objective of the Sustainable Development Goals. This would be more evident when we look at the India's Disability Act, 2016.

The Nature of Disability and the Right of Persons with Disabilities Act, 2016 of India

The Right of Persons with Disabilities Act, 2016 calls for a comprehensive understanding of the subject. It starts with conceptual clarification on *Persons with Disabilities.* Under the Right of Persons with Disabilities Act, 2016 of India, "person with disability" means a person with long term physical, mental, intellectual or sensory impairment which, in interaction with barriers, hinders his full and effective participation in society equally with others.

Further, disability has been classified under two broad categories:

1. **Physical disability** includes:

   A. Locomotor disability including (*a*) "leprosy cured person", (*b*) "cerebral palsy", (*c*) "dwarfism", (*d*) "muscular dystrophy", and (*e*) "acid attack victims";
   B. Visual impairment includes (*a*) "blindness"and (*b*) "low-vision";
   C. Hearing impairment includes (*a*) "deaf" and (*b*) "hard of hearing"; and
   D. "speech and language disability".

2. **Intellectual disability**, includes : (*a*) "specific learning disabilities", and (*b*) "autism spectrum disorder".

Understanding the world of Disability enables us to educate internally of their sufferings from various infirmities, both physical and intellectual, and that they deserve special care and attention for fulfilling their earthly quality of life as human being.

As mentioned earlier, as per the Census 2011, there are 2.68 crore Persons with Disability (PwD) in India constituting 2.21 per cent of the total population. This, however, could be an underestimate because according to the World Health Organisation, 15 per cent of the world's population faces some form of disability. Social stigma being the reason of under reporting has to be addressed by the local governments for meeting their special needs under SDGs.

In this given background, it would be worthwhile to look at programme interventions of the Ministry of Social Justice and Employment, the nodal ministry for the PwDs in India.

Programme Initiatives and Outlays for the Persons with Disabilities in India

The Government of India in the Ministry of Social Justice and Empowerment created on 12 May, 2015 the Department for Empowerment of Persons with Disability for building an all-inclusive society in which equal opportunities are provided for both growth and development of Persons with Disability so that they can lead productive, safe and dignified life. Its Mission is to empower Persons with Disability, through various Acts/ Institutions/Organizations and Schemes for rehabilitation and to create an enabling environment, that provides such persons with equal opportunity, guarantees protection of their rights and enables them to participate as independent and productive member of the society. In order to realize this Vision and achieve Mission, the Department strives for the following objectives:

(a) Undertaking following measures for rehabilitation:
   (i) Physical rehabilitation, which includes early detection and intervention, counselling, medical rehabilitation, and assistance in procuring appropriate aids and appliances for reducing the effect of disability;
   (ii) Educational rehabilitation;
   (iii) Economic rehabilitation including vocational education; and
   (iv) Social empowerment;
(b) Developing rehabilitation professionals/personnel;
(c) Improving Internal Efficiency/Responsiveness of Service Deliveries; and
(d) Advocating empowerment of Persons with Disability through awareness generation among different sections of the society.

Table 5.6: Budgetary flow of Fund and Expenditure for Persons with Disabilities

Year	Budget Estimate	Revised Estimate	Actual Expenditure
2011-12	480.00	334.70	292.02
2012-13	500.00	261.24	223.90
2013-14	550.00	460.00	341.49
2014-15	565.00	375.00	337.96
2015-16	565.40	540.00	487.19
2016-17	700.00	695.00	675.00

Source: Plan Expenditure Report of the Department of Empowerment of Persons with Disabilities, (2011-12 to 2016-17).

Given the fact that a separate department was created for focused services, it would be apt to look at performances for delivery of services since 2011-12. The Department's website as on 14 November, 2019 mentions the following (Table 5.6) with respect to planned Expenditure Report of the Department of Empowerment of Persons with Disabilities:

The Expenditure Report is a valuable indicator of the volume of fund that was spent for the PwDs and the government's social commitment for the vulnerable *vis-à-vis* aggregate load of required services for the different categories of PwDs and its population size. However, the size of the actual expenditures, over the years, when compared with the size of PwDs population, as Table 5.4 does not inspire much comfort, leaving a signal that more has to be done. Further, in absence of any physical output/data of the reach of beneficiaries, it is impossible to have any fair idea of the un-bridged gap that exists among the various categories of PwDs. Be that as it may, let us see also the latest budgetary provision for various categories of PwDs for the year 2019-20.

The website of the Ministry of Social Justice and Empowerment (Department of Empowerment of Persons with Disabilities), as on 5th November, 2019 mentions that under Demand No. 92, the following programmes have been put in place with fund, as noted in Table 5.7.

Table 5.7: Policy support: Programmes for the PwDs during 2019-20

Name of the programme	Schemes under the programme	Outlay for the year 2019-20 (in Rs. crores) for each of the programme	Unit of measurement indicator	Target for the year 2019-20
1.Assistance to Disabled person for purchase/Fitting of Aids/Appliances (AIDP)	1. Affordable assistive devices available different types of disabilities	230.00	1.1 No. of beneficiaries	3, 00, 000
	2. Financial outlays for distribution of aids and assistive devices		2.1 No. of female beneficiaries	82, 000
	3. Organizing distribution camps for aids and assistive devices		3.1 No. of SC beneficiaries	52, 480

(*Contd.*)

Name of the programme	Schemes under the programme	Outlay for the year 2019-20 (in Rs. crores) for each of the programme	Unit of measurement indicator	Target for the year 2019-20
	4. Promoting awareness of the scheme		4.1 No. of ST beneficiaries	26,240
2.Information and Mass Education	1. Implement information and mass education activities aimed at welfare and empowerment of PwDs	28.00	1.1 Number of electronic media campaigns undertaken	5
			1.2 Number of print media campaigns (advertisements to be published) undertaken	50
			1.3 Number of screens in outdoor media campaigns	50
			1.4 Number of social media posts	500
			1.5 Number of events/fairs participated	10
			1.6 Number of creatives designed (including documentaries, TVC, microdocs, radio jingles, audio spots etc.)	8
3. Deendayal Disabled Rehabilitation Scheme (DDRS) (CS)	1 Assistance to NGOs/ Projects	75.00	1.1 Number of beneficiaries (General category)	30375
			1.2 Number of SC beneficiaries	6750
			1.3 Number of ST beneficiaries	3375

(Contd.)

Name of the programme	Schemes under the programme	Outlay for the year 2019-20 (in Rs. crores) for each of the programme	Unit of measurement indicator	Target for the year 2019-20
			1.4 Number of NE beneficiaries	4500
			1.5 Percentage of SwDs who dropout from school	6%
	2. Disbursal of grants		2.1 Number of districts covered	250
	3. Improved coverage of disabilities through projects		3.1 Beneficiaries with intellectual disability	27000
			3.2 Beneficiaries with mental illness	200
			3.3 Beneficiaries with Hearing impairment	11000
			3.4 Beneficiaries with Visually impairment	5000
			3.5 Beneficiaries with Leprosy cured Persons	800
			3.6 Beneficiaries with Cerebral Palsy	900
			3.7 Beneficiaries with Speech & Language Disability	100
4. Support to Establishment/ Modernization/ Capacity augmentation of Braille Press (CS)	1. Establishment of new Braille presses in states	8.00	1.1 Number of Braille pages printed	1.5 cr pages
	2. Establishment of small units of Braille press in UTs		—	—
	3. Continuing support to existing Braille presses			

(*Contd.*)

Name of the programme	Schemes under the programme	Outlay for the year 2019-20 (in Rs. crores) for each of the programme	Unit of measurement indicator	Target for the year 2019-20
5. Support to National Trust (CS)	1. To benefit persons with autism, cerebral palsy, intellectual disability and multiple disabilities	20.00	1.1 No. of Persons with disabilities provided Health Insurance cover	100000
			1.2 Day care services to inmates of 'Disha & Vikaas' Centres	6000
			Residential services to inmates of 'Samarth' & 'Gharaunda' centres	3000
			1.4 Mainstream of school education	1000
6. Setting up in State Spinal Injury Centre (CS)	1. Establishment of centres for providing free treatment and management of spinal injury	5.00	1.1 Number of patients rehabilitated	73
7. Indian Spinal Injury Centre (CS)	1. Benefiting persons with spinal injuries of the economically weaker sections by supplementing expenditure on treatment and management of spinal injury	4.00	1.1 Number of patients rehabilitated	95
8. Establishment of Colleges for Deaf (CS)	1. Enhanced capacity of deaf and dumb colleges in five regions	3.00	1.i Number of hearing-impaired students enrolled in colleges for graduation	60
			1.2 Number of degrees awarded to hearing impaired students	**

(*Contd.*)

Name of the programme	Schemes under the programme	Outlay for the year 2019-20 (in Rs. crores) for each of the programme	Unit of measurement indicator	Target for the year 2019-20
			2.1 Number of students placed in employment post-completion of the course	**
			2.2 Average remuneration of students placed in employment post-completion of the course	**
9. Scholarship for Students with Disabilities (CS)	1. Empower female students with disabilities (SwDs)	125.00	1.1 Number of students provided scholarships (General category)	23100
			1.2 Number of SC students provided scholarships	5600
			1.3 Number of ST students provided scholarships	2800
			1.4 Number of North Eastern students provided scholarships	3500
			1.5 Number of female students provided scholarships	10500
			1.6 Number of Pre-Matric scholarships awarded	14000
			1.7 Number of Post-Matric scholarships awarded	20075

(*Contd.*)

Name of the programme	Schemes under the programme	Outlay for the year 2019-20 (in Rs. crores) for each of the programme	Unit of measurement indicator	Target for the year 2019-20
			1.8 Number of Top Class scholarships awarded	220
			1.9 Number of National Overseas scholarships awarded	5
			1.10 Number of Fellowships awarded	200
			1.11 Number of Free Coaching scholarships awarded	500
	2. Awareness generation among and sensitization of various stakeholders		2.1 Percentage of beneficiaries dropping out (To be provided subject to availability from NSP and/ or MHRD)	**
	3. Timely disbursement of funds			
10. Schemes for Implementation of Persons with Disabilities Act (CS)	(a) Accessible India Campaign: 1. Public building made accessible to PwDs for casing access to service	315.00	1.1 Percentage of public buildings to be made accessible (out of total 1662 buildings)	**15% i.e. 200 buildings Approximately
	2. Website made accessible to PwDs for easing access to information		2.1 Percentage of websites to be made accessible through ERNET (out of 917 websites)	45% i.e. 400 websites Approximately

(Contd.)

Name of the programme	Schemes under the programme	Outlay for the year 2019-20 (in Rs. crores) for each of the programme	Unit of measurement indicator	Target for the year 2019-20
	(b) Skill training	1. Provide quality skill training	1.1 No. of beneficiaries placed/ employed	21000
			1.2 Increase in number of employers participating in Placements	65
		2. Identification of training curriculam for new job roles suitable for PwDs		-
		3. Increase in participation of women with disabilities		-
		4. Enhanced mobility and performance of PwDs under skill training programmes		-
	(c) Awareness Generation and Publicity	1. Creating awareness and sensitization about schemes and programmes for PwDs	1.1 No. of sensitization programmes through government agencies	10
			1.2 No. of sensitization programmes through NGOs	20
			1.3 No. of participants expected	5000

(Contd.)

Name of the programme	Schemes under the programme	Outlay for the year 2019-20 (in Rs. crores) for each of the programme	Unit of measurement indicator	Target for the year 2019-20
	(d) In-service training and sensitization:	1. Release of grants for training and sensitization of key functionaries in the Central/State governments about the scheme and provision for PwDs	1.1 Number of beneficiaries	4000

Source: The website of the Ministry of Social Justice and Empowerment (Department of Empowerment of Persons with Disabilities), as on 5th November, 2019.

The focus of the ministry and the department, as per their Vision and Mission appears to be the Act, and budgetary provisions have been accordingly made. On its perusal, it will also appear that volume of PwDs of different categories, spread over rural and urban areas need more inclusive and robust programme interventions. All the PwDs need to be brought under person-specific support programme. Such PwDs need not wait in the queue for uncertain delivery of services. In the spirit of Sustainable Development Declaration, they deserve priority accommodation. Needless to mention, the SDGs are more than and beyond the Act; it aims at inclusive outreach and development of all, and that no PwDs would remain left behind. For that matter, periodical report of the coverage of PwDs under different sections of the Act are as important as coverage under identified goal areas. Moreover, the periodical report of coverage under the Act would also be inputs for validation of the performances by the high end indicators of the related SDGs.

Sustainable Development Goal Approach of India vs. the Right of Persons with Disabilities Act, 2016 of India

The Sustainable Development Summit envisaged 'a world free of poverty, hunger, disease and want, where all life can thrive— A world where we reaffirm our commitments regarding the human right to safe drinking water and sanitation where there is improved hygiene; and where food is sufficient, safe, affordable and nutritious.' The Sustainable Development Summit resolved to create conditions for sustainable, inclusive and sustained economic growth, shared prosperity and decent work for all, taking into different levels of national development and capacities. Also a just, equitable, tolerant, open and socially inclusive world in which the needs of most vulnerable are met through programme interventions. The Act centred programme intervention is rather restrictive and does not enjoy the broader view and perspective of the new global agenda of Sustainable Development Goals, including the supreme agenda that nobody should be left behind'.

This boils down to impose on us to undertaking a new framework of programme interventions for taking the *Persons with Disabilities 6 of India in a different development pathway to reach the destination journey*. It is a common understanding and usual practice of any government system that a general programme of life support and incidental necessities meant for all would also be able to take care of special needs of the vulnerable. The history and development experiences suggest that the implementation of common general programme seldom reaches to the vulnerable and voiceless social group and that a dedicated Sub-Plan is needed to be structured for them. In other words, an dedicated programme strategy and planning has to be in place for ensuring outcome under SDGs for the persons with disabilities.

Sub-Plan on Persons with Disabilities

The Sustainable Development Summit envisaged a world of universal respect for human rights and human dignity, the rule of law, justice, equality and non-discrimination and at Para 19 and at Para 23 of its Declarations, it has reiterated to respect, protect and promote human rights and fundamental freedoms for all including the persons with disabilities who happen to be the most vulnerable and need to be covered fully and comprehensively. This largely uncared marginalized section of our society, living mostly in underdeveloped and developing countries, require to be lifted from 'curse of fatalism' and sub-human existence through massive, robust and focused programme support of new hope and new meaning of life through a dedicated Sub-Plan of their own. One of the finer tests of SDGs really fulfilling its core objective would be in terms of success of outreach and outcome for this special category of physically challenged and mentally retarded population. This Sub-Plan needs to focus on Education, Accessible schools, Employment, Inclusiveness, Accessible Transport and Accessible public places. However, since all the 17 Sustainable Development Goals are meant for all persons, including persons with disabilities, care has to be taken that such vulnerable section is adequately and comprehensively covered under other SDGs as well, including No poverty, Social protection, Health coverage, Sexual and reproductive health and access to water and sanitation as well.

Based on the rights of the Persons with Disabilities (PwDs) and also to meet their human development deficit, both in rural and urban areas of developed and developing countries, a Sub-Plan for PwDs has to be in place for focused intervention, a model of which is given hereunder.

For effective implementation of any scheme, Outcome Matrix is a handy tool for ensuring whether the production process starts with required inputs, both physical and financial, that jump start a host of activities the end product of which lead to output. Outcome is obtained when outputs are appropriately made use of, and based on quality of such outcome, the impact of any programme is finally assessed. Since the final outcome of programme efforts never come auto-generated, it cannot be realised unless the process is monitored at every stage of the process. Because of the very nature of person-specific programme intervention for persons with disabilities, it calls for collaborative partnership of guardians/friends during the monitoring process. There is, therefore, critical role of the parents' bodies to ensure that person-specific disabilities are taken into consideration for treatment, care, rehabilitation, means of livelihood, life-support, protection and the like. Needless to

Table 5.8: Model Sub-Plan for the Persons with Disabilities

Sustainable Development Goals	Heads of Development	Minor Heads of Development	Targets of Sustainable Development	Indicators to be addressed	Programme interventions by the country Government	Proposed Outlay for the Financial Year—*
I	No Poverty	1. Reduction in Poverty for all. 2 Social Protection System for all	1.2 Reduction in Poverty 1.3 Social Protection System	1.2.2 1.3.1		
II	Zero hunger	1 Nutrition security to all 2 Malnutrition redress	2.1 Nutrition security 2.2 Ending Malnutrition	2.1.1 2.2.1, 2.2.2		
III	Good health & well-being	7. Universal coverage of essential health services & vaccines	3.8 Universal health coverage	3.8.1		
IV	Quality Education	5. No disparities on gender, disability and other grounds 7. Access & Basic facilities for sustainable life style and development	4.5 Access to Education & Vocational Training 7.1 Sustainable life style development	4.5.1 4.7.1		
V	Gender Equality	1. No Discrimination against women and girls. 2. No Violence against all women and girls, including trafficking 3. No Child Marriage, including harmful practices.	5.1 Ending Discrimination against Girl Child 5.2 Violence against Girl Child 5.3 Elimination of harmful practices and Child Marriage	5.1.1 5.2.1 & 5.2.2 5.3.1		

(*Contd.*)

Sustainable Development Goals	Heads of Development	Minor Heads of Development	Targets of Sustainable Development	Indicators to be addressed	Programme interventions by the country Government	Proposed Outlay for the Financial Year—*
VI	Clean water & Sanitation	1. Access to safe drinking water for all 2. Access to adequate sanitation and hygiene for all	6.1 Access to safe drinking water 6.2 Access to equitable Sanitation & Hygiene	6.1.1 6.2.1		
VIII	Decent work and Economic Growth	5. Full and productive employment and decent work for all women and men	8.5 Decent Work	8.5.1 & 8.5.2		
X	Reduced inequality	2. Social, economic and political inclusion of all	10.2 Empowerment	10.2.1		
XI	Sustainable cities and Communities	2. Access to safe, affordable, accessible and sustainable public transport systems for all 5. Public spaces for all	11.2 Public Transport system to be PwD—friendly 11.7 Access to public spaces	11.2.1 11.7.1 & 11.7.2		

mention that stakeholders should be actively involved, as far as possible, to design a Sub-Plan of their own 'future' along with its implementation.

Conclusion

The out-reach programme under SDGs for the Persons with Disabilities has yet to achieve sufficient momentum, and country-specific achievements on different categories of persons with disabilities are yet to be discernible or visible. For ensuring that this vulnerable sub-group receives adequate attention and that nobody is left behind, the scope of capturing annual progress through Voluntary National Reviews (VNR) could be tried to speed up programme efforts for the Persons with Disabilities.

6
Relooking the Approach towards the Women

The Declaration of Sustainable Development Goals is a momentous event in shaping the destiny of our planet by way of transforming our world to build a better future for all people and to achieve their full human potential. The SDG Summit Declaration is a call for action to change our world with a global agenda for the next 15 years. It envisioned "to end poverty and hunger everywhere; to combat inequalities within and among countries; to build peaceful, just and inclusive societies; to protect human rights and promote gender equality and the empowerment of women and girls; and to ensure the lasting protection of the planet and natural resources."

The Sustainable Development Goals is built upon, among other things, the premises of the Universal Declaration of Human Rights as well as other international instruments relating to human rights and international law. It focused on the realization that gender equality and the empowerment of women and girls will make a crucial contribution to progress all the goals and targets. It declares that the achievement of full human potential and of sustainable development is not possible if one-half of humanity continues to be denied its full human rights and opportunities. It maintains that women and girls must enjoy equal access to quality education, economic resources and political participation as well as equal opportunities with men and boys for employment, leadership and decision making at all levels. It also required the systematic mainstreaming of a gender perspective in the implementation of the Agenda. Before addressing the 'Achieve gender equality and empower all women and girls of Sustainable Development Goal-5', let us quickly look back the perspective, including the decisions of the four world conferences on women that lead to the adoption of SDG-5.

Historical Journey of Women Development

The abiding importance and realisation of gender inclusive development has not been a sudden jerk or of any kind of momentary decision at the Sustainable Development Summit, 2015. It was in fact a culmination of interventions that started as far back as 1945 with the founding of United Nations Charter where a provision for equality between men and women was enshrined (Chapter III, article). The female officials within the United Nations and leaders of women's movements on the global stage did their part to shape it into action until 1975, but with not very uniform responses. However, with the passing of a United Nations General Assembly resolution that 1975 should be observed as International Women's Year, and a further resolution (resolution-31/138) that 1976-1985 should be the "Decade of Women", the women mainstreaming in social and economic development got a stable platform.

Accordingly, the UN Commission on the 'Status of Women' called the first world conference on women in Mexico in 1975 to coincide with the International Women's Year that resulted the Declaration of Mexico on the Equality of Women and Their Contribution to Development and Peace—a World Plan of Action for the Implementation of the Objectives of the International Women's Year for the advancement of women through 1985.

The Second World Conference on Women was held in Copenhagen in 1980. It reviewed progress in implementing the goals of the Women in first world conference and noted the gap between rights being secured for women and women's ability to exercise those rights and reiterated equal access on employment, health and education as set out in Mexico. It called for Programme of Action for stronger national measures to ensure women's ownership and control of property, as well as improvements in protecting women's rights to inheritance, child custody and nationality.

The Third World Conference to Review and Appraise the Achievements of the UN Decade for Women was held in Nairobi in 1985. It set out areas in which progress in women's equality could be measured—in Constitutional provisions and legal systems, additionally in equality in social participation, equality in political participation and decision-making areas. The Conference concluded that women need to participate in all areas of human activity at the national level, not just those areas that relate to gender.

The Fourth World Conference on Women in 1995 held in Beijing was a significant turning point for the global agenda for gender equality. The Beijing Declaration and Platform for Action centred on agenda for women's empowerment and recognised as the key global policy document on gender equality. It sets strategic objectives and actions for the gender equality in 12 critical areas, namely Women and Poverty, Education and Training of Women, Women and Health, Violence against Women, Women and Armed Conflict, Women and the Economy, Women in Power and decision-making, Institutional Mechanism for the Advancement of Women, Human Rights of Women, Women and the Media, Women and the Environment and the Girl-child,

The Beijing Platform for Action and its Follow-up

The Platform for Action is an agenda for women's empowerment and of the principle of shared power and responsibility between women and men at home, in the workplace and in the wider national and international communities. Equality between women and men is a matter of human rights and a condition for social justice and is also a necessary prerequisite for equality, development and peace. A transformed partnership based on equality between women and men is a condition for people-centred sustainable development. It also reaffirms the fundamental principle adopted by the World Conference on Human Rights, that the human rights of women and of the girl child are an inalienable, integral and indivisible part of universal human rights throughout their life cycle.

The UN Division for Women, in its review of the Fourth World Conferences, stated "The fundamental transformation that took place in Beijing was the recognition of the need to shift the focus from women to the concept of gender, recognizing that the entire structure of society, and all relations between men and women within it, had to be re-evaluated.

The implementation of the Beijing Declaration and the Platform for Action have been assessed by the UN Commission on the status of women each year and through a review process carried out every five years, reaffirming strong commitment to its full implementation, the first of such review having held at the General Assembly in 2000 followed by 10-Year Review in 2010 when it also voiced for speedier implementation of Millennium Development Goals The 15-Year review took place in 2010 when it called for the full and accelerated implementation of the Beijing Declaration and Platform for Action. Incidentally, an important step in 2010 was also the establishment of another UN expert mechanism dedicated to women's rights, namely the United Nations Working Group on discrimination against women and girls (WGDAW), set up by the UN Human Rights Council in 2010. Finally, the 20-Year review and appraisal in 2015 noted the progress made towards achieving gender equality, in providing a strong basis for the full, effective, and accelerated implementation of the commitments made in Beijing, and also addressed opportunities for achieving gender equality and the empowerment of women in the post-2015 development agenda.

The Sustainable Development Summit, 2015 took note of aspirations, shortcomings, challenges, its current status, the women rights, the decisions of UN Human Rights Commission etc. in framing the new global development agenda—the 2030 Agenda for Sustainable Development. The new global agenda also integrated gender component in all its sustainable goals. Further, the achievement of gender equality and the empowerment of all women and girls was also posted as stand alone Goal No. 5. It is noted for the first time in its targets 5.1 and 5.2 on the elimination of all forms of discrimination and violence against women and girls in the public and private spheres.

Sustainable Development Summit, 2015 and its Declaration on Women

The Sustainable Development Summit, 2015, in its historic declaration observed that Gender inequality remains still a key challenge even after 15 years of the Millennium Development Goals in place. It took note of MDGs achievement of lifting up hundreds of millions of people from extreme poverty and put in place increased access to education for both boys and girls. However, maternal, newborn and child health and reproductive health remain off-track. The Summit made a clarion call to recommit to the full realization of all off-track Millennium Development Goals. The Summit, 2015 reaffirmed that gender equality and the empowerment of women and girls will make a crucial contribution to progress across all the Goals and targets. The achievement of full human potential and of sustainable development is not possible if one half of humanity continues to be denied its full human rights and opportunities. Women and girls must enjoy equal access to quality education, economic resources and political participation as well as equal opportunities with men and boys for employment, leadership and decision-making at all levels. It will work for a significant increase in investments to close the gender gap and strengthen support for institutions in relation to gender equality and the empowerment of women at the global, regional and national levels. The systematic mainstreaming of a gender perspective in the implementation of the Agenda is crucial.

In other words, the sustainable development goals seek to change the course of the twenty first century, addressing key challenges such as poverty, inequality, and violence against women. Women's empowerment is a pre-condition for this Empowering women and girls to reach their full potential requires that they have equal opportunities to those of men and boys. This means eliminating all forms of discrimination and violence against them, including violence by intimate partners, sexual violence and harmful practices, such as child marriage and female genital mutilation (FGM). Ensuring that women have better access to paid employment, sexual and reproductive health and reproductive rights, and real decision-making power in public and private spheres will further ensure that development is equitable and sustainable. Additionally, women have a critical role to play in all of the SDGs, with many targets specifically recognizing women's equality and empowerment as both the objective, and as part of the solution. Goal 5 is known as the stand-alone gender goal because it is dedicated to achieving these ends.

Based on the above perspective, the Goal 5 of the SDGs—**Achieve gender equality and empower all women and girls**, as designed, are noted below along with its targets and related indicators:

Goal 5. Achieve Gender Equality and Empower all Women and Girls

5.1 End all forms of discrimination against all women and girls everywhere.

5.2 Eliminate all forms of violence against all women and girls in the public and private spheres, including trafficking and sexual and other types of exploitation.

5.3 Eliminate all harmful practices, such as child, early and forced marriage and female genital mutilation.

5.4 Recognize and value unpaid care and domestic work through the provision of public services, infrastructure and social protection policies and the promotion of shared responsibility within the household and the family as nationally appropriate.

5.5 Ensure women's full and effective participation and equal opportunities for leadership at all levels of decision-making in political, economic and public life.

5.6 Ensure universal access to sexual and reproductive health and reproductive rights as agreed in accordance with the Programme of Action of the International Conference on Population and Development and the Beijing Platform for Action and the outcome documents of their review conferences.

5a. Undertake reforms to give women equal rights to economic resources, as well as access to ownership and control over land and other forms of property, financial services, inheritance and natural resources, in accordance with national laws.

5b. Enhance the use of enabling technology, in particular information and communications technology, to promote the empowerment of women.

5c. Adopt and strengthen sound policies and enforceable legislation for the promotion of gender equality and the empowerment of all women and girls at all levels.

The goals and targets *per se* are important from the angle of programme vision and intended outcome. However, from the perspective of monitoring the performance, indicators do play critical role on two counts: first it acts as a management tool to help countries develop implementation and monitoring strategies for achieving the SDGs and to monitor progress, and secondly, it works as a report card, to measure progress towards achieving a target and ensure the accountability of governments to their citizens and adopt sound national sustainable development policies. The Global Indicator Framework as designed by the UN Statistical Commission at its 47th Session in March 2016 and adopted thereafter by the Economic and Social Council and the General Assembly, are as follows:

Monitoring Indicators of Sustainable Development Goal-5

5.1.1 Whether or not legal frameworks are in place to promote, enforce and monitor equality and non-discrimination on the basis of sex.

5.2.1 Proportion of ever-partnered women and girls aged 15 years and older subjected to physical, sexual or psychological violence by a current or former intimate partner in the previous 12 months, by form of violence and by age.

5.2.2 Proportion of women and girls aged 15 years and older subjected to sexual violence by persons other than an intimate partner in the previous 12 months, by age and place of occurrence.

5.3.1 Proportion of women aged 20-24 years who were married or in a union before age 15 and before age 18.

5.3.2 Proportion of girls and women aged 15-49 years who have undergone female genital mutilation/cutting, by age.

5.4.1 Proportion of time spent on unpaid domestic and care work, by sex, age and location.

5.5.1 Proportion of seats held by women in (a) national parliament and (b) local governments.

5.5.2 Proportion of women in managerial positions.

5.6.1 Proportion of women aged 15-49 years who make their own informed decisions regarding sexual relations, contraceptive use and reproductive health care.

5.6.2 Number of countries with laws and regulations that guarantee full and equal access to women and men aged 15 years and older to sexual and reproductive health care, information and education.

5.a.1 (a) Proportion of total agricultural population with ownership or secure rights over agricultural land, by sex; and (b) share of women among owners or rights-bearers of agricultural land, by type of tenure.

5.a.2 Proportion of countries where the legal framework (including customary law) guarantees women's equal rights to land ownership and/or control.

5.b.1 Proportion of individuals who own a mobile telephone, by sex.

5.c.1 Proportion of countries with systems to track and make public allocations for gender equality and women's empowerment.

Gender Issues in Related SDGs

The Goal-5 of the SDGs is, however, not be all and end all of gender issues under SDGs. All the SDGs are meant for all people, including the women. The gender issues have been interwoven under all the other Sustainable Development Goals to ensure that one-half of the humanity does not miss the development radar. Thus SDG-1 of No Poverty mentions to focus on eradication of extreme poverty and vows to measure proportion of women below the international poverty line, reduce at least half the proportion of women and children of all ages according to national definition by 2030, implement nationally appropriate social protection systems by appropriate coverage. At SDG-2 of nutritional security, it is to ensure safe, nutritious and sufficient food all year round and address the nutritional needs of adolescent girls, pregnant and lactating mothers. The SDG-3 of universal health speaks of reduction of maternal mortality ratio to less than 1 lakh live births, access to sexual and reproductive health care services and universal health coverage. The SDG-4 mentions about free, equitable and quality primary and secondary education for girls and ensure affordable and quality technical, vocational and tertiary education including university. The SDG-6 requires to ensure universal and equitable access to safe and affordable drinking water and sanitation for all. The SDG-7 also mentions access to affordable, reliable, sustainable and modern energy for all. The SDG-8 is to put in place productive employment and decent work for women, secure proportional informal employment in non-agricultural employment and ensure equal pay for work of equal value and protect against exploitation of women in work scenario. The SDG-10 speaks of reduction of inequality within and among countries. The SDG-16 mentions access to justice for all.

A Summary View of the Women in India

The Census of India captures the status of women from demographic angle according to which female population on 2011 stood at 58.65 crore, registering 48.9 per cent of India's population with sex ratio of 943. This is the highest sex ratio recorded since 1971 though the child sex ratio declined in 2011 over 2001 from 927 to 914, and that decline in rural India is more than the drop in urban India in 2011. The literacy rates for females was found at 65.46 per cent as against the males at 82.14 per cent. Interestingly, out of total 20,17,00,941 literates added during the decade, female addition of 11,00,69,001 outnumber male addition of 1,07,631, 940. This improvement of female literacy in more than males has been found in both in rural and urban areas. The gender gap in literacy has thus come down from 21.59 to 16.68 percentage points in 2011. As per the Sample Registration System (SRS) Bulletin of Registrar General of India (RGI), the Infant Mortality Rate (IMR) has reduced from 37 per 1,000 live births in 2015 to 30 per 1,000 live births in 2019 at National Level and the Maternal Mortality Rate (MMR) has reduced from 8.1 in 2015-17 to 7.3 in 2016-18 at National Level. The Ministry of Health & Family Welfare released Compendium of Factsheets on NFHS-5 (2019-21) which revealed the status of women in India, a part of which is captured hereunder.

Table 6.1: Factsheets on NFHS-5 (2019-21)

Sl.No.	Indicators	Urban	Rural	Total
1.	Female population age 6 years and above attended school (%)	82.5	66.8	71.8
2.	Women with 10 or more years of schooling (%)	56.3	33.7	41.0
3.	Women who ever used the internet	51.8	24.6	33.3
4.	Women age 20-24 years married before age 18 year of age (%)	14.7	27.0	23.3
5.	Total Fertility Rate	1.6	2.1	2.0
6.	Women age 15-19 years who were already mother or pregnant at the time of survey (%)	3.8	7.9	6.8

(*Contd.*)

Sl.No.	Indicators	Urban	Rural	Total
7.	Neo-natal mortality Rate (NNMR) (Per 1000 live births)	18.0	27.5	24.9
8.	Infant Mortality Rate (IMR) (Per 1000 live births)	26.6	38.4	35.2
9.	Under 5 Mortality Rate (U5MR) (Per 1000 live births)	31.5	45.7	41.9
10.	Women whose bodymass index (BMI) is below normal<18.5kg/m2 (%)	13.2	21:2	18.7
11.	Women who are overweight or obese BMI>__25.0kg/m2(%)	33.2	19.7	24.0
12.	All women age 15-49 years who are anaemic (%)	53.8	58.5	57.0
13.	All women age 15-19 years who are anaemic (%)	56.5	60.2	58.1
14.	Currently married women who usually participate in three household decisions (%)	91.0	87.7	88.7
15.	Women who worked in the last 12 months and were paid in cash (%)	25.0	25.6	25.4
16.	Women having a house and/or land (alone or jointly with others) (%)	38.3	45.7	43.3
17.	Women having a mobile phone that they themselves use (%)	69.4	46.6	54.0
18.	Ever married women age 18-49 years who have ever experienced spousal violence (%)	24.2	31.6	29.3
19.	Ever married women age 18-49 years who have ever experienced physical violence during any pregnancy (%)	2.5	3.4	3.1
20.	Young women age 18-29 years who experienced sexual violence by age 18 (%)	1.1	1.6	1.5

Source: Factsheets on NFHS-5 (2019-21).

Women Rights in India

Women rights are given appropriate recognition to end the gender based inequities, reducing disparity between men and women, improving socio-economic status of women and increasing their participation in various fields. A set of women-friendly legislations are in place to ensure that women gain equal rights, opportunities and access to resources. The legal safeguards so provided are through the Articles of the Constitution of India and other Acts passed by the Parliament. They are as follows:

A. **Constitutional Provisions:** The Constitution of India has provided rights of women to ensure gender equality under:
   - Article 14: For Equality before Law,
   - Article 15(3): Prohibition of discrimination on grounds of religion, race, caste, sex or place of birth,
   - Article 39A: For Equal Justice and free legal aid,
   - Article 42: Provision for just and humane conditions of work and maternity relief, and
   - 73rd-74th Amendment of the Constitution mandating 33 per cent reservation for women in the local governance.

B. **Legislative Provisions:** The Parliament has also passed a host of legislations for protection of women and mandating women's rights, namely,
   - The Pre-Conception and Pre-Natal Diagnostics Act (PCPNDT), 1994,
   - The Protection of Women from Domestic Violence Act, 2005,
   - The Dowry Prohibition Act, 1961,
   - The Indecent Representation of Women (Prohibition) Act, 1986,
   - The Sexual Harassment of Women at Workplace (Prevention, Prohibition and Redressal) Act, 2013,
   - The Prohibition of Child Marriage Act, 2006,
   - The Minimum Wages Act, 1948,
   - The Equal Remuneration Act, 1976,
   - The Maternity Benefit (Amendment) Act, 2017, and
   - The Criminal Law (Amendment) Act 2013, making the punishment more stringent for offences like rape, sexual assaults etc.

NITI Aayog and the Intervention Strategy on SDG-5

NITI Aayog has been the forum for the adoption and monitoring of the SDGs in the country. It tasked itself for initiating the SDGs intervention in the country. Accordingly, NITI Aayog in consultation with MoSPI prepared a draft, mapping of the goals and targets as an initial step. Additionally, it undertook the mapping of the centrally sponsored schemes, including central sector schemes, that have been already in place and classifying/grading them as the 'core of the core', 'core' and 'optional' scheme implemented by the States and aligned with one or more SDGs. This mapping has been summarized hereunder.

Table 6.2: SDG-5 Achieves gender equality and empower all women and girls

Sl. No.	SDG Targets	Centrally Sponsored Schemes/Central Schemes	Concerned Department
5.1	End all forms of discrimination against all women and girls everywhere	1. Mission for Protection and Empowerment of Women (Beti Bachao Beti Padhao, Pradhan Mantri Mahila Shakti Kendra (PMMSK), One Stop Centre, Women Helpline, Hostels, SWADHAR Greh, gender budgeting etc.)	* Schemes 1to 4 administered by WCD
		2. Pradhan Mantri Matru Vandana Yojana (PMMVY)	
		3. Umbrella ICDS	
		4. Supporting Training and Employment Programme (STEP)	
		5. National Scheme for Incentive to Girl Child for Secondary Education	* Schemes 5 and 6 administered by HRD
		6. Pragati (Providing Assistance for Girls' Advancement in Technical Education)	

(*Contd.*)

Sl. No.	SDG Targets	Centrally Sponsored Schemes/Central Schemes	Concerned Department
5.2	Eliminate all forms of violence against all women and girls in the public and private spheres, including trafficking and sexual and other types of exploitation	1. Mission for Protection and Empowerment of Women [Beti Bachao Beti Padhao, Pradhan Mantri Mahila Shakti Kendra(PMMSK), One Stop Centre, Women Helpline, Hostels, SWADHAR Greh, gender budgeting etc.]	* Schemes 1 and 2 administered by WCD
		2. Umbrella ICDS	
5.3	Eliminate all harmful practices, such as child, early and forced marriage and female genital mutilation	1. Mission for Protection and Empowerment of Women (Beti Bachao Beti Padhao, Pradhan Mantri Mahila Shakti Kendra (PMMSK), One Stop Centre, Women Helpline, hostels, SWADHAR Greh, Gender budgeting etc.)	* Schemes 1 and 2 administered by WCD
		2. Umbrella ICDS	
5.4	Recognize and value unpaid care and domestic work through the provision of public services, infrastructure and social protection policies and the promotion of shared responsibility within the household and the family as nationally appropriate	1. Mission for Protection and Empowerment of Women	* Schemes 1 administered by WCD
		2. Pradhan Mantri Ujjala Yojana	* Schemes 2 administered by Petroleum and Natural Gas Department
		3. Labour and Employment Statistical System	* Schemes 3 administered by Labour Department
5.5	Ensure women's full and effective participation and equal opportunities for leadership at all levels of decision-making in political, economic and public life	1. Rastriya Gram Swaraj Yojana (RGSY)	* Schemes 1 administered by Panchayati Raj Department

(*Contd.*)

Sl. No.	SDG Targets	Centrally Sponsored Schemes/Central Schemes	Concerned Department
5.6	Ensure universal access to sexual and reproductive health and reproductive rights as agreed in accordance with the Programme of Action of the International Conference on Population and Development and the Beijing Platform for Action and the outcome documents of their review conferences	1. National Health Mission	* Schemes 1 and 2 administered by Health & FW Department
		2. National AIDS Control Mission	
		3. Pradhan Mantri Matru Vandana Yojana (PMMVY)	* Schemes 3 administered by WCD
5.a	Undertake reforms to give women equal rights to economic resources, as well as access to ownership and control over land and other forms of property, financial services, inheritance and natural resources, in accordance with national laws	1. Deen Dayal Antyodaya Yojana (DAY)—National Rural Livelihood Mission (NRLM)	* Schemes 1 administered by RD
		2. Deen Dayal Antyodaya Yojana (DAY)—National Urbal Livelihood Mission (NULM)	* Schemes 2 administered by Housing & Urban Development
		3. Pradhan Mantri Jan Dhan Yojana	* Schemes 3 administered by Finance, Land Resources and WCD

(*Contd.*)

Sl. No.	SDG Targets	Centrally Sponsored Schemes/Central Schemes	Concerned Department
5.b	Enhance the use of enabling technology, in particular information and communications technology, to promote the empowerment of women	1. Science and Technology Institutional and Human Capacity Building	* Schemes 1 administered by S&T, Telecommunication, WCD and Dei TY
5.c	Adopt and strengthen sound policies and enforceable legislation for the promotion of gender equality and the empowerment of all women and girls at all levels	1. Mission for Protection and Empowerment of Women (Beti Bachao Beti Padhao, Pradhan Mantri Mahila Shakti Kendra (PMMSK), One Stop Centre, Women Helpline, Hostels, SWADHAR Greh, Gender budgeting etc. 2. Gender Budgeting	* Schemes 1 administered by WCD * Schemes 2 administered by Social Justice & Empowered Department.

Source: 21 Mapping of Sustainable Development Goals, August 2018, NITI Aayog, New Delhi (File No.F-20019/PA-SDGs/2017-DMEO-Part(1).

The schemes mapped by NITI Aayog indicate to show that India has addressed the functional areas of Goal-5 through programmes of the departments of government. The NITI Aayog also mentioned that the aforesaid schemes go in some ways to address cross-cutting issues of SDG-2, SDG-3, SDG-4, SDG-6, SDG-7, SDG-8, SDG-9/SDG-10 and SDG-16 for women empowerment. While such mapping has been important for the initial stage to link on-going schemes with the new agenda and goals of SDGs, it never qualified as the real or permanent intervention strategy. All the schemes were designed with different programme objectives and targets of earlier years, as distinct from SDG vision of 'nobody should be left behind'. Besides, implementation format of such programmes do not address outcome as designed for monitoring indicators of SDGs. In fact, neither the NITI Aayog nor the departments ever worked on efficacy and its extent on these on-going programmes to meet the high valued goals and targets of

SDG-5. However, several new schemes have been added since the starting of SDGs on first January, 2016. The updating of mapping of the SDGs by inclusion of new schemes, target-wise, has yet to take place at the level of NITI Aayog.

Major Women Development Schemes in India

A good number of schemes on women development, protection and empowerment have been in place for the women of the country as a whole under different ministries of the Government of India. The exact number of such schemes varied with passage of time. It is about 147 schemes, big and small, that are now being administered by different ministries of the Government of India. Additionally, several state governments have designed their state-specific women empowerment schemes. The objectives of major schemes of the departments of the Government of India have been to empower women in multiple ways in areas of security, access to the government or local authorities to address their concern and issues, for ensuring proper care of their children while in jobs and also to enhance their skill for earning opportunities etc. A short list of such schemes is shown below :

(a) *Against Violence*

1. Beti Bachao Beti Padhao Scheme (BBBP): Beti Bachao Beti Padhao Scheme, introduced in 22nd January, 2015, is a campaign of the Government of India to address female foeticide, gender discrimination and the declining child sex ratio in India. The name Beti Bachao, Beti Padhao translates to 'Save the girl child, educate the girl child'. The scheme aims to ensure survival, protection and education of girl children and educate citizens against gender bias and improve the efficacy of welfare services for girls. The key elements of the scheme include Enforcement of PC & PNDT Act, nation-wide awareness and advocacy campaign and multi-sectoral action in select 100 districts, with low Child Sex Ratio in the first phase. It was launched with initial funding of Rs. 100 crore.

2. One Stop Centre Scheme (OSCs): The One Stop Centre provides support and assistance to women affected by violence, both in public and private spaces, within the family, community and work places. Women facing physical, sexual, emotional, psychological and economic abuse, irrespective of age, class, caste, education status, marital status, race and culture will be facilitated with support and redressal. It is a centrally sponsored scheme and is funded through the Nirbhaya fund. State governments receive 100 per cent Central assistance to protect women affected by violence (such as acid attacks, rape, and sexual harassment) in public and private spaces. This scheme facilitates emergency (medical), legal aid and counselling, non-emergency services under one roof to combat all forms of violence against women. In case girls under 18 years of age are referred to the Centre, they will also be served in coordination with authorities/institutions established under Juvenile Justice (Care and Protection of Children) Act, 2000 and Protection of Children from Sexual Offence Act, 2012.

(b) *For Protection*

1. SWADHAR Greh: SWADHAR Greh, envisions a supportive institutional framework for women victims of difficult circumstances to regain their emotional strength that gets hampered due to their encounter with unfortunate circumstances. This Government of India scheme for women's empowerment aims to provide shelter, food, clothing, social, economic and health security. It also provides legal assistance to them, helps them take initiative for readjusting in societies and rehabilitate them economically and emotionally. Under the Scheme, Swadhar Greh is intended to be set up in every district with capacity of 30 women.

2. Women Helpline Scheme: Women Helpline Scheme is one of the government schemes for women empowerment that intends to give 24×7 emergency responses to women affected by violence in private or public spaces. The universalisation of women helpline number has been done in every State and Union Territory through a single toll-free number (181) that provides immediate support to women nationwide. Further, this scheme creates awareness about women empowerment schemes and programmes.

3. Mahila Police Volunteers: The Ministry of Women and Child Development, along with Home Affairs, launched the Mahila Police Volunteers scheme in all States and Union Territories. This Central Government-sponsored scheme aims to create a link between police authorities and local communities to ensure police outreach on crime cases. This scheme works to create a safe woman-friendly environment and encourages women to join the police force.

4. Working Women Hostel: The Working Women Hostel scheme is intended to promote availability of safe and conveniently located accommodation for them with day care facility wherever possible in urban, semi-urban or even rural areas where employment opportunities exist. Children of working women, up to the age of 18 years for girls and up to the age of 5 years for boys may be accommodated in such hostels with their mothers.For this women empowerment scheme, the Government provides grant-in-aid for construction and new hostel buildings and extension of an existing building in rented premises.

5. National Crèche Scheme: The Government has introduced National Crèche Scheme for the children of a working mother. This scheme provides daycare facilities to the children and guarantees to improve the health and nutrition status of children. Further, this women empowerment intervention promotes physical, social, and holistic development of children and educates parents to enhance childcare methods or techniques.

(c) *For Empowerment*

1. STEP (Support to Training and Employment Programme for Women): One of the most effective women empowerment schemes in India is STEP (Support to Training and Employment Programme for Women). It was introduced to provide training in skill development and to assure employment to women. This government-backed scheme offers grants to institutions and organisations to conduct the training programme.

2. Mahila Shakti Kendras (MSK): Another popular women empowerment scheme in India is Mahila Shakti Kendra. It aims to provide one-stop convergent support services to women to develop skills, generate employment opportunities, and increase digital literacy. This scheme is operational at multiple levels, such as national level, state level, and district level. The Government intends to cover the 115 most backward districts by establishing 920 Mahila Shakti Kendras.

3. Mahila E-Haat: Mahila E-Haat is an initiative of the Ministry of Women and Child Development which provides an opportunity for women entrepreneurs for using technology and presents their products (made/manufactured/sold) on an online platform. With only mobile and internet connections, women entrepreneurs can showcase their products along with descriptions and photographs. Here, buyers can also reach sellers telephonically, physically, through email or any other medium. The list of products may include clothing, fashion accessories, pottery, boxes, home décor, toys and many other things. This initiative supports the 'Make in India' programme through an online platform.

The Global Gender Gap Report and India

The annual Global Gender Gap Report (GGGR) of the *World Economic Forum* (WEF) gives comprehensive data based on four key dimensions, namely—economic participation and opportunity, educational attainment, survival and health, and political empowerment to showcases gender parity in comparison to their positions in the previous year indicating whether the countries have progressed or plummeted in terms of gender equality.

The Global Gender Gap Report 2022 published in July 2022, shows that out of 146 countries, *India is placed at 135,* while in 2021 India had ranked 140 out of 156 countries, India scored 0.629 in 2022, which indicates an increment of 0.003 from last year when it scored 0.625. The position of Sub-Indexes are also shown in Table below:

Table 6.4: Global Gender Gap (GGG) Report, India

Index/Sun-Index	**2022 (out of 146 countries)**		**2021 (out of 156 countries)**	
	Rank	**Score**	**Rank**	**Score**
Global Gender Gap Index	135	0.629	140	0.625
Political empowerment	47	0.257	51	0.276
Economic participation and opportunity	143	0.350	151	0.376
Educational attainment	107	0.961	114	0.962
Survival and health	146	0.937	155	0.937

Note: On each of the four sub-indices as well as on the overall index the GGG index provides scores between 0 and 1, where 1 shows full gender parity and 0 is complete imparity.

The Minister of Women and Child Development Government of India, in a written reply in Lok Sabha on 17 December, 2021 on Global Gender Gap Report 2021 stated that Indian score has come down largely due to Political Empowerment dimension. India's score in this dimension should be one of the highest in the world as India has provided 30 per cent reservation to women at local self-government level and representation of women in the local self-government bodies is more than 30 per cent at present. However, the publishing agency, World Economic Forum, takes into account representation of women in Parliament only. It has further mentioned that Government of India has given utmost priority to bridge the gender gap in India, reducing disparity between men and women, improving the health of women, increasing their socio-economic status and participation in various fields. Some major initiatives taken by Government of India for removing the gender gap in all aspects of social, economic and political life are as follows:

Economic Participation

- Beti Bachao Beti Padhao ensures the protection, survival and education of the girl child.

- Scheme for Adolescent Girls aims to empower girls in the age group 11-18 and to improve their social status through nutrition, life skills, home skills and vocational training.
- Working Women Hostel ensures the safety and security for working women.
- The National Crèche Scheme ensures that women take up gainful employment through providing a safe, secure and stimulating environment to the children.
- Pradhan Mantri Awaas Yojana aims to provide housing under the name of the woman also.
- Pradhan Mantri Kaushal Vikas Yojana aims to enable a large number of Indian youth including women to take up industry-relevant skill training in securing a better livelihood.
- Deen Dayal Upadhyay National Urban Livelihoods Mission focuses on creating opportunities for women in skill development, leading to market-based employment.
- Sukanya Samriddhi Yojana—Under this scheme girls have been economically empowered by opening their bank accounts.
- Skill Upgradation & Mahila Coir Yojana is an exclusive training programme of MSME aimed at skill development of women artisans engaged in Coir Industry.
- Prime Minister's Employment Generation Programme is a major credit-linked subsidy programme aimed at generating self-employment opportunities through establishment of micro-enterprises in the non-farm sector.
- Pradhan Mantri Mudra Yojana provides access to institutional finance to micro/small business.

Education

- Samagra Shiksha Scheme *inter alia* has provisions of gender segregated toilets in all schools and teachers' sensitization programmes to promote girls' participation, Rani Laxmi Bai

Atmaraksha Prashikshan and stipend for girl children with special needs.

- Kasturba Gandhi Balika Vidyalayas (KGBVs) have been opened in educationally backward blocks for girls belonging to disadvantaged groups.
- University Grants Commission (UGC) and All India Council for Technical Education (AICTE) are implementing various fellowship/scholarship schemes. 159 Women Studies Centres have been established in various Universities and Colleges to undertake research and develop curricula in the areas of gender equity, economic self-reliance of women, girls' education etc. In order to improve Gender Balance in Undergraduate Programmes in IITs, 5039 supernumerary seats for female students have been created since 2018-19.

Health and Nutrition

- Government has announced Mission Poshan 2.0 to strengthen nutritional content, delivery, outreach and outcomes with focus on developing practices that nurture health, wellness and immunity to disease and malnutrition.
- Pradhan Mantri Matru Vandna Yojana aims to provide maternity benefit to pregnant and lactating mothers.
- Implementation of Reproductive, Maternal, Newborn, Child, Adolescent Health plus Nutrition (RMNCAH+N).
- Rollout of Comprehensive Primary Health Care including health promotion through Ayushman Bharat-Health & Wellness Centres (AB-HWC).
- Janani Shishu Suraksha Karyakaram (JSSK) to eliminate out-of-pocket expenses for pregnant women delivering in public health institutions and sick infants accessing public health institutions for treatment.
- Janani Suraksha Yojana (JSY) to provide financial assistance to pregnant women for encouraging institutional delivery.

- Surakshit Matritva Aashwasan (SUMAN) to provide assured, dignified, respectful and quality healthcare at no cost and zero tolerance for denial of services.
- Pradhan Mantri Surakshit Matritva Abhiyan (PMSMA) to provide comprehensive and quality ANC to pregnant women on the 9th of every month.
- Laqshya initiative to improve the quality of care in Labour room and Maternity Operation Theatres.
- Pradhan Mantri Ujjwala Yojana empowers women and protects their health by providing LPG cylinder free of cost.

Political Participation

- To bring women in the mainstream of political leadership at the grassroots level, government has reserved 33 per cent of the seats in Panchayati Raj Institutions for women. Capacity Building of Panchayat Stakeholders including Elected Women Representatives is conducted with a view to empowering women to participate effectively in the governance processes.

Gender Budget in India in Relation to SDG-5

Budget is a financial plan for implementation of priority programmes of a country in a given year, while Gender budgeting is used as a tool to reform gender inequality, outcome oriented allocation and expenditure, and secure socio-economic development to make sure that gender gap is systematically reduced and that the benefits of development reach women just as much as men. Gender budget have come in vogue in India from the year 2005 when India started releasing a gender budget statement along with its Union budget. The Gender Budget Statement comprises two parts:

- Part A reflects Women Specific Schemes, i.e. those which have 100 per cent allocation for Women.
- Part B reflects Pro Women Schemes, i.e. those where 30 per cent of the allocation is for Women.

Following the (erstwhile) Planning Commission guidelines in 2010, the Government of India has since been using the revised concept, Gender Responsive Budgeting (GRB) or Gender Budgeting. Gender responsive budgeting (GRB) brings together two issues that were not commonly associated with one another: gender equality and public financial management. GRB argues that gender equality principles should be incorporated into all stages of the budget process.

In a very brief overview, India's Gender Budget has increased from Rs. 24,241 crore in 2005-06 to Rs. 1,43,462 crore in 2020-21, registering a six-fold increase in absolute terms, with allocations as a proportion to the total budget between 4.3 per cent and 5.9 per cent. The allocation was less than 5 per cent of the total budget in five of the last six years. The Gender Budget for 2021-22 was posted at Rs. 1,53,326 while the 17th Gender Budget in 2022-23 allocated Rs. 11,71,006.47 crore, an increase of 11.5 per cent. Despite country's big vision, the quantum of 2022-23 year's Gender Budget continued to remain less than 5 per cent, like its previous year, 2021-22. However, as a proportion of total expenditure, the Gender Budget has declined 4.4 per cent to 4.3 per cent.

Under Part A of the Gender Budget 2022-23, it has been allocated Rs. 26,772.89 crore, increased by six per cent from the last year budget of Rs. 25,260.96, which covered schemes such as Nirbhrya Fund, Saksham Anganwadi and Poshan 2.0, SAMARTYA and SAMBAL (part of Mission Shakti encompassing Beti Bachao Beti Padhao, Creche, Pradhan Mantri Matru Vandana Yojana) among others. Part B of the allocation has increased a hike of 12 per cent compared to 2021-22, increasing from Rs. 1,28,749.83 to Rs. 1,44,233.50 crore which included among others Samagra Shiksha, Flexible Pool for Reproductive and Child Health (RCH) and Health System Strengthening, National Health Programme and National Urban Health Mission, Pradhan Mantri Awas Yojana (Urban), Mahatma Gandhi National Rural Employment Guarantee Scheme, to name a few.

The scope and magnitude of gender budgeting in India have come under severe attacks both from the women groups and also from the academicians raising questions on broad methodology of budget preparation. The fundamental systemic issue that has been raised against gender budgeting is the basis on which schemes are included or excluded and also the need of a very defined criteria on inclusion of schemes under Part A or Part B. It has also been pointed that some big schemes like Jal Jeevan Mission (JJM) that benefit a good section of women has not come under gender budgeting at all. It is also maintained that there is hardly any good logic for exclusion of schemes that earmark less than 30 per cent of their funds for women in the gender budgeting. The way schemes allocate at least 30 per cent of their funds for women also seems unclear and that the lack of gender-segregated data leaves a gaping hole for an effective GRB. Meaningful allocations in Part B, specifically, becomes difficult in the absence of disaggregated gender data. It is for this reason some scholars have pointed out that the entire process has become an aggregation exercise rather than a potent tool. It is also held that the GRB lacks focus on gender parity and that it has not turned out to be effective instrument for ensuring outcome to meet gender gap and bring gender justice.

Professor Lekha Chakraborti of the National Institute of Public Finance and Policy (NIPFP) observed that while the gender budgeting was started as an ex-post policy analysis of the Union Budget through a gender lens, it has given a framework to integrate future-centric programme design and budgeting favouring women. She cited the example of schemes providing clean fuel to women in poor income households. It has been maintained by others that despite its shortcomings, the Gender Budget has succeeded in drawing attention to gender issues. "One of the biggest achievements of gender-responsive budgeting is the mainstreaming of the idea that a gender lens is important within the fiscal discourse."

Gender Budgeting for Sustainable Development Goals

The GRB exercise has also to be looked not only from gender parity and gender-gap perspective but, more importantly, from the necessity of funding the implementation of Sustainable Development Goals. Earlier, the Sustainable Development Summit observed that sustainable development is only possible when women and girls enjoy equal access to quality education, economic resources as well as equal opportunities with men and boys for employment, leadership and decision making at all levels. In other words, the systemic mainstreaming of a gender perspective in the implementation of Sustainable Development Agenda is crucial. Here lies the importance of gender budgeting for SDGs. Thus, there is necessity of providing funding support for meeting annual targets of SDG-5 of gender equality and empowerment keeping in mind its monitoring goals. The budgetary support is also called for all other SDGs linked with broader objectives of SDG-5, especially those of SDG-1 (No Poverty), SDG-2 (Zero Hunger), SDG-3 (Good Health & Well-being), SDG-4 (Quality Education), SDG-6 (Clean Water and Sanitation), SDG-7 (Affordable Clean Energy), SDG-8 (Decent Work and Economic Growth), SDG-10 (Reduced Inequalities) and SDG-16 (Peace, Justice and Strong Institutions). It is critical that appropriate programmes have to be drawn and budgeted for to release fund for implementation. However, GRB in India is less empowered in that it does not address existing gender gap in listed sectors or provide funding support schemewise for SDG-5 or other SDGs linked with women empowerment. It has turned out to be mere ritualistic. Incidentally, the history and development experiences suggest that the implementation of common general programme seldom reaches to the vulnerable social group and that dedicated programmes with budgetary support are needed for the outreach and outcome.

Given the current approach of India towards gender-just system, it will take considerable time to bridge gender gap in socio-economic development. A commentator jocularly said that India will need 195 years to close gender gap! There is no denying the fact that India is rather slow towards achieving a gender-just world of equality of men and women. Gender equality is both a necessary and sufficient condition for inclusive growth. Unless programme interventions are made as per studied gaps on SDG-5 and other linked SDGs with required budgeted fund, it would be well-nigh impossible to reach the destination journey at 2030.

7
Reordering the Approach towards the Older Persons

Elderly or old age consists of ages nearing or surpassing the average life span of human beings. Aging is a pattern of life that changes as one grows older. The biological and psychological aging usually occur gradually, over years and therefore, there is no single age at which people in general can be said to be old. However, people older than 60 are usually called 'old or aged'. The size of aged population of the world or for any country has been on the rise. The international concerns for the problems faced by the older persons got noticed and the First World Conference on Ageing took place at Vienna convened by the UN General Assembly in 1982 which called for specific action on such issues as health and nutrition, protecting elderly consumers, housing and environment, family, social welfare, income security, and employment, education. In 1991, the General Assembly adopted the United Nations Principles for Older Persons in Madrid, enumerating 18 entitlements for older persons— relating to independence, participation, care, self-fulfilment and dignity. The Plan of Action called for changes in attitudes, policies and practices at all levels to fulfil the enormous potential of ageing in the twenty-first century. Its specific recommendations for older persons include actions for health and well-being and ensuring enabling and supportive environments.

There were about 901 million people aged 60 years and above in the worldover in 2015, at the time of SDG Summit which were projected to grow by 56 per cent at 1.4 billion in 2030, registering 16.5 per cent of the global population. The special needs of older generation like different kinds of nutrition, health care and other livelihood support came up. The sustainable development Agenda, 2030 seeks to realize human rights for all segments of the society, at all ages, including older persons, in a life cycle approach. It took note of cultural divide between the old and others in many parts of the world. The Sustainable Development Summit Declaration calls for protecting and promoting the rights of older generations through the 2030 Agenda with ageing, cutting across the goals on poverty eradication, good health, gender equality, economic growth and decent work, reduced inequalities and sustainable cities and to go beyond treating older persons as a vulnerable group. Older persons must be recognized as the active agents of societal development in order to achieve truly transformative, inclusive and sustainable development outcomes.

The Elderly or Old Persons in India

The National Policy for Older Persons adopted by the Government of India in 1999 defines elderly persons of those aged 60 or more. Based on the said cut off age of 60 or more, there were about 103.8 million older persons as per 2011 Census of India representing 8.6 per cent of the population Earlier, the 2020 National Commission on Population report estimated that there will be nearly 138 million elderly persons in India in 2021, comprising 67 million males and 71 million females. Strikingly, the growth rate of the elderly population is higher than that of the general population. While the general population has grown by 18 per cent in 2001-2011 and estimated 12.4 per cent in 2011-2021, the elderly population has grown almost by 36 per cent each in the two decades. As a result, the proportion of the elderly in the general population has increased.

Programmes and Schemes for the Elderly in India

The NITI Aayog is the nodal agency of the country for all programme activities connected with SDGs, including the vulnerable, like the Aged. The schemes mapping of the NITI Aayog, however, follows goal-wise pattern and do not specifically highlight them for the vulnerable. Therefore, for the vulnerable aged segment of population, it has to be found out from the websites of the Social Justice & Empowerment Department and also of others.

(a) The Ministry of Social Justice & Empowerment

The Ministry of Social Justice & Empowerment is the nodal Ministry for the welfare of the aged in India. However, interventions of the Ministry on the old care programmes are not outcome to the response of the declaration of Sustainable Development Goals, but reflect as a general call on welfare duties of the government. It seeks to address the problems of the aged from two angles—(a) regulatory and (b) promotional.

Regulatory

Regulatory actions are taken by means of legislations which empowers designated functionaries to operationalize them with the state machinery. The first regulatory Act is known as Maintenance and Welfare of Parents and Senior Citizens Act, 2007. It seeks to ensure need-based maintenance for Parents and Senior Citizens and their welfare.

Promotional

Promotional activities are developmental in nature and tries to address multiple problems of the aged through linked programme/schemes. The websites of the Ministry of Social Justice & Empowerment delineated a host of such schemes meant for the aged. It mentions about National Action Plan for the Welfare of Senior Citizens which needs to capture Senior Citizens' Home for 25 destitute senior citizens to provide food, care and shelter, Senior Citizens Home for 50 Elderly Women including those under

Sansad Adarsh Gram Yojana (AAGY), Continuing Care Home and Homes for Senior Citizens affected with Alzheimer's disease/ Dementia for a minimum of 20 Senior Citizens who are seriously ill, Mobile Medical Care Units to provide medical care to Senior Citizens living in rural, isolated and backward areas, Physiotherapy clinics for Senior Citizens for a minimum of 50 Senior Citizens per month and Regional Resources & Training Centres (RRTCs) to provide technical support. For facilitating desirable optimum output, it mentions about convergence with initiatives of other Ministries/Departments in Government of India in the field of Senior Citizens Welfare (CWMSrC) and Media Advocacy, Capacity Building, Research or Study Pilot and other projects through NISD (National Institute of Social Defence). It also notes about. Rashtriya Vayoshri Yajona (RVY) Scheme for providing Physical Aids and Assisted-living Devices for Senior Citizens (free of cost to Citizens of BPL Category), Senior Citizens Welfare Fund and National Council of Senior Citizens.

(b) Other Ministries

The Finance Ministry takes care of financial burden of the aged and provides various exemption facilities for senior citizens and very senior citizens for Income tax payment and also exempts interest income from bank/post office deposits. The Ministry of Road Transport and Highways provides facilities of reservation of two seats for senior citizens in front row of the buses of the State Road Transport Undertakings. The Ministry of Railways provides Fare concession in all Mail/Express including Rajdhani/Shatabadi/ Jan Shatabadi trains for senior citizens, aged Female 58 years and Male 60 years and above. The element of concession is 40 per cent for Male and 50 per cent for female. Indian Railways also have the facility of separate counters for Senior Citizens for purchase/ booking/cancellation of tickets. Wheel Chairs for the use of older persons are available at all junctions, District Headquarters and other important stations for the convenience of needy persons including the older persons. Ramps for wheel chairs movement are available at the entry to important stations. The Air India under the Ministry of Civil Aviation provides air fare concession up to 50 per cent of basic fare of normal economy class for senior citizens who have completed 60 years of age. The Ministry of Consumer Affairs, Food and Public Distribution, under the Antyodaya Scheme, provides older persons of the Below Poverty Line (BPL) families with food grains at the rate of 35 kgs. per family per month. The food grains are issued at the rate of Rs. 3 per kg. for rice and Rs. 2 per kg. for wheat. Moreover, under the Annapoorna Scheme being implemented by the States/UT Administration, 10 kgs. of food grains per beneficiary per month are provided free of cost to those senior citizens who remain uncovered under the old age pension scheme.

State Action Plan for Senior Citizens (SAPSrC)

Chapter 5 of the Maintenance and Welfare of Parents and Senior Citizens Act, 2007 provides for "Protection of Life and Property of Senior Citizens". Since "Police" and "Public order" are state subjects, the respective State Governments are required to draw a comprehensive Action Plan for providing protection of life and property of senior citizens and take measures to ensure safety and security and elimination of all forms of neglect, abuse and violence against old persons through initiatives such as identification of senior citizens; sensitization of police personnel regarding safety, security of older persons; regular visit of the beat staff; setting up of toll free senior citizen helpline; setting up of senior citizen security cell; verification of domestic helps etc.

The Current Status of the Elderly Persons in India

The Social Statistics Division at the National Statistical Office (NSO) of the Government of India published in August 2021 the fifth *Elderly in India* which brought out some interesting features of the elderly in India. On 'Old age dependency ratio', defined as the number of elderly people per 100 persons between the ages of 15-59, it grew from 10.9 per cent in 1961 to 14.2 per cent in 2011, and is projected to increase further to 15.7 per cent in

2021—quoting the population data of the National Commission on Population. Moreover, NSO's National Sample Survey (NSS) data from 2017-18 reveals that 70 per cent of the elderly in India were dependent on others for their daily living. The situation was worse for females—only 10 per cent and 11 per cent of females were economically independent in rural and urban areas respectively, compared to the 48 per cent and 57 per cent of males in rural and urban areas. The NSO's report *Periodic Labour Force Survey 2018-19* reveals that the participation of those aged 60-64 in economic activities has fallen from 49.3 per cent in 2011-12 to 40.9 per cent in 2018-19. About 72 per cent of men and 21 per cent of women of this age group participated in economic activities in rural areas, and 51 per cent of men and 10 per cent of women in urban areas.

Further, in both urban and rural areas, the proportion of elderly females participating in unpaid domestic work is almost twice that of males. However, the proportion of elderly females participating in paid employment activities is far less than that of males.

On important heath burdens of the Aged, as per the 76th round of the NSS conducted in 2018, the most common disability among the elderly is locomotor disability (5.5%) followed by hearing disability (1.6%) and visual disability (1.4%). The occurrence of the latter two is slightly higher in rural as compared to urban areas. More than 50 per cent of elderly persons suffering from a disability—other than mental illness—have consulted doctors and are undergoing treatment.

Additionally, according to 2019 data from the Ministry of Home Affair's National Crime Records Bureau, the highest crime rate per lakh population for offences committed against the elderly were found in Delhi (93.8% crimes), whereas states like Assam, Jammu and Kashmir, Jharkhand, Meghalaya and Uttarakhand, reported rates of less than one crime per lakh population.

The National Policy of the Older Persons *versus* the Sustainable Development Goals for the Aged

The National policy of the Older Persons, 1999 was a follow-up action of the UN General Assembly Resolution 47/5 to observe the year 1999 as the International Year of older persons keeping in furtherance of the Directive Principles of State Policy as enshrined in Article 41 of the Constitution of India. The National Policy on Older Persons (NPOP), 1999 envisages State support to ensure financial and food security, health care, shelter and other needs of older persons, equitable share in development, protection against abuse and exploitation, and availability of services to improve the quality of their lives. The policy also covers issues like social security, intergenerational bonding, family as the primary caretaker, role of Non-Governmental Organizations, training of manpower, research and training.

The National Policy for the Older Persons, 1999 was revised in 2011 to take care of new challenges of the ageing population with implications at the national) level and household level. The new policy, styled as the "National Policy for Senior Citizens, 2011 was adopted by taking cognizance of demographic explosion among the elderly, the changing economy and social milieu, advancement in medical research, science and technology and higher level of destitution among rural poor. A higher proportion of elderly women than men experience extreme loneliness and dependent on children. The new policy addresses issues concerning senior citizens living in rural and urban areas along with special needs of the 'oldest old' and older women. The New National Policy aims at income support, subsistence security and other cares in old age through Indira Gandhi National Old Age Pension Scheme, Public Distribution System, revised Income Tax slab, access to Microfinance, improved Healthcare, positioning broadened Safety and Security measures and visible protection, access to. Housing, Productive Ageing, expansion of other welfare care services for the old age and Multigenerational bonding. The media has been perceived to be used as instrument to promote dissemination of services. The new policy also addresses special needs during natural disasters or similar kind of emergencies. It embodies in details implementation mechanism of the new policy.

The Sustainable Development Goals delineates specified items for the care of aged, Goal-wise for its appropriate address by the country governments at various levels. While all the goals are interconnected and meant for the older persons as well, some goals, as mentioned hereafter, are inescapably necessary and need to be made available to older persons as entitlement. SDG-1 (No Poverty) mentions about eradication of poverty for all and also putting in place of social protection system for all. SDG-2 (Zero Hunger) focuses on Nutrition security to all and also on malnutrition redress. SDG-3 (Good Health and Well-being) speaks of universal coverage of essential health services and vaccines. SDG-4 (Quality Education) says about Lifelong Learning opportunities. SDG-5 (Gender Equality): Older women tend to be more marginalized and disadvantaged than older men, and face higher rates of poverty. SDG-8 (Decent Work and Economic Growth) mentions about the scope of participation of older person's in the labour market. SDG-10 (Reduced Inequalities) speaks of opportunities of social, economic and political inclusion of all. SDG-11 (Sustainable Cities and Communities) says about providing safe, affordable and sustainable transport for all; as well as universal access to safe, inclusive and accessible, green and public spaces.

The National Policy for Senior Citizens, 2011 adopted the international concern of the older persons prevalent during the preceding years in the forum of the Madrid Plan of Action and the conferences of United Nations, including the Macau Outcome Document 2007. The SD Summit, 2015 took notes of all past internal conventions and conferences, and based on new vision of sustainable development, declared a new charter of development for the people, planet, prosperity, peace and partnership, to ensure that all human beings can fulfil their potential in dignity and equality and in a healthy environment within a measurable destiny target period of 2030. The interventions sought under SDGs are naturally more robust and comprehensive to secure sustainable living for all older persons—rural or urban, male or female, organized or unorganized. As a matter of fact, the national policy for senior citizens/older persons needs to be reworked and updated in the light of SDGs.

Revisiting the Grey Areas of the Policy on Senior Citizens, 2011

The central focus of the Sustainable Development Goals is inclusive development. In the context of older persons, the SDG declaration means that all the eligible older persons of varying ages living in rural, urban or relatively inaccessible areas would have to be the recipients of delivery of services. It means that list of such older persons along with all relevant personal data need to be captured at the first instance and then made available to field level functionaries to work out particular package of services needed by them and then made it available. This is a huge task for a bigger country like India with ever increasing elderly population, and that a database, location-wise, for each of older persons, has to be created to start with. This calls for a new statistical and monitoring system. The idea that no one should be left behind is also contingent upon having a statistical system in place to monitor even for the last older person eligible to be beneficiaries of related schemes designed under-related SDGs. Incidentally, around the world, the statisticians have been working at warp speed to set up mechanism to deliver the much needed data for the SDG services. The integration of geospatial information and statistical data is very crucial for an effective system. This is a big challenge for the policy reforms in India for proper monitoring of SDG services meant for the older persons.

The services meant for the older persons under SDGs can broadly be divided under two broad categories: Group specific and person specific, though they are not mutually exclusive. Group specific programme are meant those schemes/projects which are common and universal in nature for all older persons. Social protection system under SDG-1. Universal coverage of essential health services and vaccines in Goal-3, Opportunities of social, economic and political inclusion in SDG-10, Safe, affordable and sustainable transport as well as universal access to safe, inclusive and accessible, green and public spaces in SDG-11 belong to common interest of all older persons. Persons-specific interventions are the most important components of old age care and account for largest volume of service seekers of the unorganized and informal sector. SDG-1(No poverty) and SDG-2 (Hunger and nutrition) belong to this category.

Understanding the areas of Implementation

The implementation mechanism decides the extent and quality of final outcome. The older persons in the country are diverse in character; it includes older groups of structured organized segments with varying degrees of old age security, for them as well as for their spouses; it also includes older persons who enjoy minimum support of post-retirement benefits; it also includes segment of persons who are left with no old age security at all. The bulk of old age persons, however, belong to the unorganised and informal sector where family dependency ratio is the highest and who face the shocks of sub-normal living. There are multitude segments of this group of older persons, male and female, living in rural or urban areas, who badly need varying services from the government for their survival, subsistence and maintenance. In fact, there is no homogeneous category of the older persons either for the organised or the unorganized sectors, and there is also no homogenous nature of person-specific service needs. For example, some section of older persons are in need of subsistence support, some segments requires special care for nutrition, while some others may need medical care or shelter. The diversity of service need is the hallmark of this vulnerable group. This diversity makes the service delivery difficult unless it is properly conceptualized and designed in the Action Plan.

There are also areas where all the older persons have commonality of service interests by and large. Access to health care facilities, access to safe, affordable and accessible public transport system, access to public space for leisure and recreation, social, economic and political inclusion, access to banking, insurance and financial services, access to safe drinking water, sanitation and hygiene etc. The macro-service requirements for the older persons are fairly representative in character and are relatively easier to handle.

This boils down to the need of identification of old age beneficiaries for specified kind of services and also specific service providers. The implementation mechanism that has been mentioned in the National Policy of Senior Citizens is that for the organized sector, the Establishments of the Government of India with the concerned ministry would be the implementing organs for delivery of services, and that a five-year perspective Plan and annual plans would be needed for setting targets and that financial allocations will be prepared by each Ministry/Department accordingly. The annual report of these Ministries/Departments will indicate progress achieved during the year. This will enable monitoring by the designated authority. Apart from the ministries of the Government of India, the concerned State Governments, other institutions/organisations and private sectors etc. do provide similar nature of old age security at the family level. While old age care is usually addressed, this segment should be kept separately as a category as it is a better serviced area. It may be designated as a premium class of old age service area. It is the uncared group that needs appropriate priority.

The Need for Old Age Security for Unorganized Older Persons

The bulk of the older persons, both male and female, staying in rural or urban areas belongs to the unorganized sector with varying diversities of service needs. In absence of uniform financial security system for older persons of this category, various State Governments have been implementing Indira Gandhi National Old Age Pension Scheme along with state-specific schemes like Old Age Pension Scheme, Widow Pension, Farmers' Pension Scheme, Fishermen's Pension Scheme, SC & ST Pension Scheme and the like. Additionally, subsistence support is given through public distribution system. There is, however, no clear picture how this category is actually being served and covered by which scheme or schemes or not being covered at all. The individual reach to the network of old age benefits does not depend as a right of entitlement but largely as ability of the individual to rope in the opportunity. The unmet needs of financial/survival security of a section of deserving older persons remains unaddressed. In a way, the extant policy and its delivery mechanism can better be described as notional and not comprehensive. This is a big challenging area for the state and other service providers and a big area for policy reform.

Need for Disaggregation and Focused Responsibility

The plurality of organisational set-ups for service delivery is an advantage in a democratic system of governance in that it helps to spread out service providers down the lines. The National Policy of Senior Persons, 2011 delineates the role of Block Development Offices, Panchayat Raj Institutions and Tribal Councils/Gram Sabhas down below. The Constitution of India under Article 243G and Article 243W, with jurisdictional items in the Eleventh and Twelfth Schedules, also enshrined functional role of the Panchayats and Municipalities to provide such service care. This apart, the Constitution also provides separate institutional mechanism for Scheduled Tribes (ST) related programmes for the Scheduled Areas under the Fifth Schedule and for the Administration of Tribal Areas under the Sixth Schedule. Additionally, Non-Governmental Organisations also provide old age support care in some areas. There exists, thus, presence of institutional mechanism for delivery of old care services, though not in uniform pattern. Shockingly, there is absence of clarity as to who will perform what kind of services by the service providers, and for what section of old age persons. Unless the disaggregated functional responsibilities among the service providers are clearly spelt out, the ultimate outcome remains vague and uncertain. The service care for the older persons would continue to suffer. This is a big policy reform area on old age service care.

Concluding Observations

'Leaving No One behind' of the older persons is not a simple task for a country like India with huge load of older population with varying diversities. Besides, priorities of a country always starts with children, youth, women and other working population, and the older persons always stand next in the queue. Besides, the statistical system of recording the growing older persons, classifying them under different segments of security requirements and organizing related support services for them are not in place. In such situation, financial implications of volume of services cannot be quantified and required fund asked for. Everything appears notional and adhoc which makes it impossible to address old care services with right focus. Since the country is far off from the uniform old age pension/ financial security of all citizens, there is no option but to segregate the relatively better off older persons of organized sector from the priority components in the Action Programme on the old ages. The searchlight of focus and attention being now on the older persons of the organized sector with reduction of income tax, interest income etc. makes the current policy less fair and equitable from macro point of view. The policy shift in favour of less privileged older persons is a call of the day with more investment and coverage which should also come under annual subject committee review of the Parliament for course correction. Such a committee report could also be the basis of country's Voluntary National Report (VNR) to the UN High Level Political Forum on Sustainable Development.

8
Revisiting the Approach towards the Scheduled Tribes

Diversity is the unique phenomenon of nature. Human species as a part of the great natural system is also unique in having rich diversity on grounds of its origin, on the influence of geographical and climatic locations, through its historical evolutionary process and also in the course of mutation of one race to another. Even though migration, immigration, biological interactions and habits and culture over time lessened the degree of diversity among the human species in general, the diversity among human stock still remains. Such diversity is conspicuously visible among the Tribal in India influenced as it is by the nature of its surroundings and its in-built social system cut off from others, being insulated to a great extent from the self-imposed local boundaries and code of its cultural habitat.

Scheduled Tribes (ST) have not been defined as such. The essential characteristics of these communities are distinguished by its *primitive traits, geographical isolation distinct culture, shy of contact with community at large and economically backwardness.* The Constitution of India under Article 366(25), however, refers to Scheduled Tribes as those communities who are scheduled in accordance with Article 342 of the Constitution which says that the Scheduled Tribes are the tribes or tribal communities or part of or groups within these tribes and tribal communities which have been declared as such by the President through a public notification.

There are various estimates about the distinct nature of such Scheduled Tribes. The Annual Report, 2010-11 of the Ministry of Tribal Welfare, however, mentions that there are over 700 Scheduled Tribes notified under Article 342 of the Constitution of India, spread over different States and Union Territories of the country. Many tribes are present in more than one state. The largest numbers of Scheduled Tribes are in the state of Odisha (i.e. 62). The Tribal groups in our country are not homogenous both on grounds of physiological factors, its regional locations and also on ground of plural socio-economic diversity; in fact the Tribal groups are at different stages of social, economic and educational development, e.g. the tribal population is relatively better placed in some North Eastern states of the country in comparisons to those of the EAG states and particularly to those 75 number known as Particularly Vulnerable Tribal Groups (earlier turned as Primitive Tribal Groups). As a matter of fact, while some tribal communities have adopted a mainstream way of life, some others like Particular Vulnerable Tribal Groups (PVTGs), at the other end of the spectrum, are still characterised by (a) a pre-agriculture level of technology, (b) a stagnant or declining population, (c) extremely low literacy, and (d) a subsistence level of economy. In fact, the PVTGs are relatively educationally and socio-economically backward, living isolated in a far away amenities and happen to be the most vulnerable among the tribals. Incidentally, the PVTG is not a constitutional concept but a Government of India classification created with the purpose of enabling improvement of low development indices. Among the 75 listed PVTGs, the *highest numbers* are found in Odisha (13), followed by Andhra Pradesh (12), Bihar including Jharkhand (9), Madhya Pradesh including Chhattisgarh (7), Tamil Nadu (6), Kerala and Gujarat having five groups each. The remaining PVTGs live in West Bengal (3), Maharashtra (3), two each in Karnataka and Uttarakhand and one each in Rajasthan, Tripura and Manipur. *All the four tribal groups in Andamans, and one in Nicobar Islands, are recognised as PVTGs.*

As per Census, 2011, there are 104281034 number of ST population in India with 23.66 per cent decadal growth and live in about 15 per cent of the country's areas, in various ecological and geo-climatic conditions ranging from plains and forests to hills and inaccessible areas in various ecological and geo-climatic conditions and constitutes about 8.6 per cent of the total population, with break-up of 11.3 per cent in rural areas and 2.8 per cent in urban areas. More than half of the Scheduled Tribes population is concentrated in the States of Madhya Pradesh, Chhattisgarh, Maharashtra, Odisha, Jharkhand and Gujarat in its plains, forests, hills and inaccessible areas. Particularly Vulnerable Tribal Groups (PVTGs) registers 32.82 per cent of ST spread across the 18 states and one UT in 2001.

Poverty Estimates of the Scheduled Tribes and Particularly Vulnerable Tribal Groups (PVTGs)

Poverty estimate is the initial step for any economic and social programme. This is particularly so when poverty reduction strategy and dedicated programme on eradication of poverty are launched. In the context of SDGs which envisages no poverty and zero hunger, the importance of the poverty estimates of the STs across regions and also among various segments of tribal population, including Particularly Vulnerable Tribal Groups (PVTGs) is paramount. Incidentally, the country does not have any updated official poverty estimates on number of ST BPL population—not to speak of region-wise and sub-category-wise poverty estimates. The poverty estimates of the bottom Particularly Vulnerable Tribal Groups (PVTGs), have also not been separately done and made available. The erstwhile Planning Commission had mentioned earlier that the population of Scheduled Tribes (ST) below poverty line has come down from 47.4 per cent in 2009-10 to 45.3 per cent in 2011-12 in rural areas. There is no separate estimates region-wise, clan-wise or for the PVTGs. Incidentally, the National Family Health Survey 2015-16 (NFHS-4) shows that 45.9 per cent of Scheduled Tribe members were in the lowest wealth bracket compared to 26.6 per cent of Scheduled Castes, 18.3 per cent of Other Backward Castes, 9.7 per cent of other castes and 25.3 per cent of those whose caste is unknown. Be that as it may, given the fact that Sustainable Development Goal-1 (SDG-1) has a new yardstick of poverty estimates—of living on less than $1.25 a day—a high per cent of ST of almost all categories, to all intents and purposes, are likely to fall in the BPL category and that livelihood support for all of them has to be provided to ensure eradication of poverty and zero hunger.

UN Sustainable Development Declarations, 2015 and Sustainable Development Goals

The UN Sustainable Development Goals (SDGs) adopted on 25th September, 2015 aimed to end hunger, assure gender equity, and build a life of dignity for all over the world. It gave a clarion call of a new framework of "Transforming Our World: the 2030 Agenda for Sustainable Development". The SDGs composed of 17 goals and 169 targets to wipe out poverty, fight inequality and tackle climate change over the next 15 years. Among the 17 goals to this agenda, focus was on complete poverty eradication, zero hunger, quality education, gender equality, sustainable cities and communities and clean water and sanitation. The 193-member General Assembly of the United Nations, headed by its Secretary General described the agenda as 'clarion call' to share prosperity, empower people's livelihood, ensure peace and heal our planet for the benefit of this and future generations. It is an agenda for the people, to end poverty in all its forms and dimensions.

The Goal-1 of Sustainable Development aims at "End poverty in all its forms everywhere". Poverty is the curse of human society. Eradicating poverty in all its forms and dimensions remains one of the greatest challenges facing the humanity and thus occupied as the central focus of Sustainable Development Goals, 2030. It is true that the MDGs initiatives brought down the number of extreme poverty by more than half in 2015, however, about 836 million people of the world still lived on less than US $ 1.25 a day. In so far as India is concerned, the erstwhile Planning Commission had earlier estimated, based on Tendulkar Methodology that 23.90 per cent of the population were reckoned as poor in 2015. The Rangarajan Committee recorded that there were 3629.29 lakhs of BPL population in India in 2011-12. The latest poverty estimate of India is to be located in "The SDG India, Index & Dashboard, 2019-20", published by NITI Aayog where referring to the World Bank's International Poverty Lines, it has been mentioned that extreme poverty in India has plummeted from 21.2 per cent in 2011 to 13.4 per cent in 2015. Multidimensional poverty also came down by half to 27.5 in between 2005-06 to 2015-16 leading to over 271 million people climbing out of poverty. Deprivations significantly reduced on all ID indicators—nutrition, child mortality, years of schooling, school attendance, cooking fuel, sanitation, drinking water, electricity, house and assets.

The macro-position of poverty status is, however, not a good indicator when looking the poverty status of the STs, a vulnerable social group in India. The SDG India, Index & Dashboard, 2019-20 did not mention separately the poverty status of the STs. In the circumstances, for the poverty status of the STs, the published document of the Ministry of Tribal Welfare would be relied on. Based on erstwhile Planning Commission's poverty estimate as per Tendulkar Methodology, the Website of the Ministry mentions that the percentage of population below the poverty line for STs during 2009-10 was 47.4 in rural areas and 30.4 in urban areas as against the national average of 33.8 per cent and 20.9 per cent respectively. In other words, there is no updated poverty status of STs at the beginning of commencement of SDGs in 2016. The requirement of sub-groupwise poverty status of STs, including PVTGs, though very relevant for addressing 'nobody should be left behind', is also not in place. This limitation needs to be kept in view while implementing 'no poverty' under goal-1.

Eradication of poverty is a big area of multi-disciplinary programme interventions. It is also interlinked with other SDGs as well, the total outcome of which would contribute to poverty reduction. However, the key area of poverty reduction is livelihood opportunities and the way such programmes are designed, implemented, monitored and ensures its outcome in a sustainable format. In this chapter, eradication of poverty of STs in India will be examined with reference to livelihood related options.

Livelihood

Livelihood is a means of supporting one's existence or of making a living financially, vocationally or otherwise. It encompasses people's capabilities, assets, income and activities required to secure the necessities of life. A livelihood is sustainable when it enables people to cope with and recover from shocks and stresses (such as natural disasters and economic or social upheavals). From human development angle, livelihood is meaningful when it meets the core of living through access, choice capabilities and participation. Access to means of living is the primary requirement; option of choice from alternative means of living is a step of moving forward. Human capabilities is also a dynamic concept and got enriched through a process of education, training and the like and seeks its realization through participation on given opportunities. This fundamental format is true for all human beings; it is true for all STs, including Particularly Vulnerable Tribal Groups (PVTGs) in our country as well.

Given the above framework of concepts, it needs to be endeavoured to find out the kind of opportunities for livelihood that exist in our country for the STs, including the Particularly Vulnerable Tribal Groups (PVTGs). The access, choice and participation depends on the kind of opportunities created by the government in this area and other programme partners. It is indeed a very crucial factor on livelihood sector since opportunities for livelihood are very often not known by the targeted audience in absence of required publicity and communication, and also on count of absence of due diligence on the part of service-providers. In making this effort, attempts need to be made to capture livelihood opportunities in the rural areas, which also covers all Particularly Vulnerable Tribal Groups (PVTGs). Dedicated schemes meant for

Particularly Vulnerable Tribal Groups (PVTGs) are very important for livelihood support and eradication of poverty.

Mapping of Livelihood Schemes

The programme interventions for livelihood options for the STs, including PVTGs are not anchored by the Ministry of Tribal Welfare. Based on rules of business of the Central Government, a good number of Central Government Ministries designs livelihood related schemes which cover the STs either directly or indirectly. Additionally, the various state governments participate in livelihood programmes either jointly in the Centrally sponsored schemes or implement their state schemes for STs. Further, under the given Constitutional framework of our country, and also based on locations of their living, the livelihood options for STs are also available from related constitutional bodies, namely,

(a) The Administration of Scheduled Areas (under the Fifth Schedule).
(b) The Administration of Tribal Areas (under the Sixth Schedule).
(c) The State Government and the related Panchayts and the Municipalities under Article 243G and 243W respectively.

The availability of various livelihood related opportunities are not universal for all categories of STs in the country as it depends on adoption of such schemes by the local government in the given area. It would have been ideal if all livelihood related options could be mapped and evaluated location-wise. However, ST related schemes of the various state governments, location specific such schemes of Scheduled Areas (under the Fifth Schedule) or of the Tribal Areas (under the Sixth Schedule) are not available in the public domain. Similarly, the ST focused schemes of the State Government nor of different tiers of Panchayats and the Municipalities are captured anywhere. In such circumstances, the mapping of livelihood related schemes of the ministries of the Central Government in one place could have been an important option to enable the stakeholders to choose livelihood option from alternatives. Even the NITI Aayog's mapping of SDG related schemes are too general to infer if such schemes are really meant for the STs for their local area as well. In other words, there is a felt need that the Ministry of Tribal Welfare need to publish, location wise, (including TSP/PESA) mapped-out list of all livelihood related schemes for SDG-1 and also for all other SDGs to ensure that such schemes are not missed out in given area on ground of lack of awareness or on count of negligence of service providers. Further, it would have enabled the stakeholders to form informed decision as to whether right type of schemes have been designed for ST on given agro-climatic and other geo-physical considerations.

Governance Issues relating to Implementation of Livelihood Programme for the Scheduled Tribes

The taste of pudding is in the eating. Thus, the schemes *per se*, though important and meaningful are not good enough unless those are implemented properly to register intended outcome. Indeed, governance issues are paramount in this outcome journey. Since there is no one to one correspondence between fund utilisation and intended outcome, the existing model of fund utilization needs a drastic overhaul to ensure outcome and inclusive growth. A new paradigm of governance has, therefore, to be put in place in meeting development deficit, more particularly of Human Development deficit of the STs, including the PVTGs.

In understanding the governance issues, it would be apt to examine at the first instance, the kind of institutional arrangements that are in place in the country for delivery of services for the STs. The institutional formats for implementing ST related programmes in the country are the following:

(a) The Scheduled Areas (under the Fifth Schedule)

The Fifth Schedule of the Constitution [Article 244(1)] deals with the administration and control of Scheduled Areas as well as of Scheduled Tribes residing in any State other than the States of

Assam, Meghalaya, Tripura and Mizoram. The Scheduled area has more than 50 per cent tribal population. It works through the Tribes Advisory Council. The Governor has the power to adapt laws passed by Parliament and State legislature in such a way that it suits these areas and make regulation for good governance and peace for the area. Further, The Panchayats (Extension to the Scheduled Areas) Act, 1996 (No. 40 of 1996) (24th December, 1996) extended the provisions of Panchayats to the tribal areas of nine states that have Fifth Schedule Areas.

(b) The Administration of Tribal Areas (under the Sixth Schedule)

The Sixth Schedule [Article 244(2)] is related to the administration of Scheduled Tribes of North Eastern States, i.e. the states of Assam, Meghalaya, Tripura and Mizoram in the North-East. It has provisions for the formation of autonomous districts and autonomous regions within the districts as there are different Schedule Tribes within the district. These autonomous districts are directly administered by the Governor. The Sixth Schedule deals with the constitution, powers and functions of District Councils and Regional Councils in these autonomous districts. The 6th Schedule areas remain within executive authority of the state.

The Indian Constitution provides funds under Article 275(1) to both Schedule Fifth and Schedule Sixth areas for the purpose of promoting the welfare of Scheduled Tribes or raising the level of administration of the Schedule Areas.

(c) The State Government for Those Living in Other Areas

The respective state government administers Scheduled Tribe related welfare schemes either directly through line departments of the state government under Tribal Sub-Plan (TSP) or through the Panchayats or Municipalities by way of devolution of powers and responsibilities under Article 243G or 243W, as the case may be.

Development Deficit for the Scheduled Tribes, including PVTGs

For any sustainable development implementation programme like SDG-1, the status of the Livelihood gaps or development deficit is the primary document based on which appropriate programme has to reach in the local area or to the individuals. Unfortunately there does not exist any ready reckoner of livelihood gap or development deficit for the STs, including PVTGs in any part of the country. Apparently, STs in general and PVTGs in particular are way below the state and national average of development indices, both as social stock and also on availability of infrastructural support to back up livelihood and other SDG programmes. These critical inputs have to be seriously addressed while working on programme intervention by the local level leaders and service providers. In the context of SDG-1, the targets and indicators have also been clearly spelt out by the Sustainable Development Summit, enabling the service providers how to go on in implementing the programme and evaluate its performance in the framework that nobody should be left behind. It goes without saying that the mapped schemes on SDG-1 would enable the local level managers to outreach services to the targeted stakeholders.

Other Governance Issues

In our democratic countries, there are multiple constitutional agencies for welfare of the STs including livelihood. The disaggregated responsibilities among such partners is crucial for outcome monitoring. Similarly, the Civil Society and the NGOs, which work on livelihood sector in Scheduled Tribe areas need to have separate identified programme and must not duplicate any efforts of other partners. For ensuring transparency of livelihood impact, convergence among programme efforts and coordination among programme partners are crucial to generate focused output at an incremental scale for the enlarged outreach. Moreover, a local campaign on availability of livelihood schemes for them through multiple communication channels, even at this stage, is absolutely necessary to create awareness, choice and participation in a transparent setting. A corollary of this initiative is the need to rebuild the cultural moor of the programme managers. Every functionary in this system is a kind of change agent for livelihood support under SDG. This value system has also to be the core of new cultural norm for the organization. This big area of SDG-ordained culture has to be visible in the organizations. Additionally, funding is the most crucial input for addressing development deficit. Accordingly, a mechanism should exist to keep records as to what extent of such funding has been made to meet the livelihood gaps of various segments of social stock in the ST areas including PVTGs.

Contingency Plan

Climate change and resultant fury of nature have been causing untold damages and sufferings by destroying significantly gains of development and built-up infrastructure. The intensity and ferocity vary from one place to another but its impact on rural and far away areas happens to be phenomenal. The STs and especially the PVTGs who stay far away at environmentally fragile zones are usually the persons who face the wrath of nature most and are hit hardest. Their poverty status gets further diminished thereafter. While a relatively developed part of the affected region with its better resource base can absorb such shocks rather easily, the living areas of STs including PVTGs find it extremely difficult to cope with the damages and even bring back its original position by way of restoration and rehabilitation. The post-calamity period of pressure and haste often searches for quick-fix solution by local agency but it seldom becomes an ideal session for rational planning. Depending on the size of any natural calamity and its assault on the SDG areas, a contingency plan for each of the SDGs, including alternative livelihood option for STs, has to be kept ready not only for compensating the loss of territory and damages, but more importantly to carry on with vigour and determination the unfinished tasks of SDGs to its destination journey.

Follow-up and Monitoring

At Para 72 of the Sustainable Development Declaration it has enjoined the importance of systematic follow-up and review to track progress in implementing the universal Goals and targets, including the means of implementation. This is very important for monitoring livelihood interventions for vulnerable social stock like the Scheduled Tribes. Since this social stock is not unique but encompasses more than 700 sub tribes that live in different agro-climatic regions and geo-physical conditions/locations and that too under different administrative jurisdictions, the scope for monitoring by a single agency is not possible. In fact it is the need of a classic case of vertical monitoring and horizontal monitoring side by side. The vertical monitoring has to be done for the given livelihood programmes of the areas by the Administration of the Scheduled Areas (under the Fifth Schedule), the Administration of Tribal Areas (under the Sixth Schedule) and the respective state government for other areas, based on transparent criteria of process monitoring and outcome monitoring. Horizontal monitoring for livelihood interventions can only be done by any agency which has overarching monitoring authority over all the administrative organs, i.e. by the NITI Aayog. It is to take care that in spite of divergent locations, there is more or less similar livelihood efforts for improvement of livelihood status. Needless to mention, the outcome monitoring would have to be done with reference to indicators designed by the Sustainable Development Summit for Goal-1 as below:

- 1.2.1 Proportion of population living below the national poverty line, by sex and age.
- 1.2.2 Proportion of men, women and children of all ages living in poverty in all its dimensions according to national definitions.
- 1.3.1 Proportion of population covered by social protection floors/systems, by sex, distinguishing children, unemployed persons, older persons, persons with disabilities, pregnant

women, new-borns, jury victims and the poor and the vulnerable.

1.4.1 Proportion of population living in households with access to basic services.

1.4.2 Proportion of total adult population with secure tenure rights to land, with legally recognized documentation and who perceive their rights to land as secure, by sex and by type of tenure.

2.1.2 Prevalence of moderate or severe food insecurity in the population, based on the Food Insecurity Experience Scale (FIES).

2.2.1 Prevalence of stunting [height for age <-2 standard deviation from the median of the World Health Organization (WHO) Child Growth Standards] among children under 5 years of age.

2.2.2 Prevalence of malnutrition (weight for height >+2 or <-2 standard deviation from the median of the WHO Child Growth Standards) among children under 5 years of age, by type (wasting and overweight).

Admittedly, this is a highly skilled professional job requiring a dedicated agency to undertake this very special category of monitoring. The NITI Aayog has to build up a network of highly skilled professional service for such monitoring around the countries.

Performance Audit

The sustainable development implementation journey needs to be faultless, driven by high moral standard of all stake-holders. The role of programme partners on the field is as important as those who oversee them at different layers. One of such off-line layers is in the forum of country's apex audit and accounts system, e.g. Comptroller & Auditor General in India. Since the SDGs will come to stay up to 2030, the apex audit body has onerous responsibility to introduce new accounting codes for all SDGs and institute performance audit. The duly validated high quality data on SDG-1, thus obtained, would enable to make reality check on 'Eradication of Poverty', its cost, performance quality and time-run of the sustainable forward journey. This would also assist outcome indicator monitoring specialists to decide how to effect concurrent/ mid-course corrections.

Conclusion

The outreach of livelihood to the Schedule Tribes including Particularly Vulnerable Tribal Groups is part of a Charter for People and Planet of the Sustainable Development Summit wherein vulnerable social group will find in the new Goals a platform to channel their infinite capacities for activism into the creation of a better world. However, the world has passed seven crucial years since the momentous declaration of Sustainable Development Goals on September, 2015. The implementation process for this great tasks in the area of SDG-1 for the STs including PVTGs, does not appear to have perceptibly galvanized. It is hoped that the commitment and combined efforts of all stakeholders would surely catch up its lost time, redouble its efforts and ensure success to the realization of 2030 Agenda of the human destiny including the eradication of poverty of Scheduled Tribes under programme efforts of SDG-1.

Appendix

Fourth World Conference on Women Beijing Declaration

Declaration

1. We, the Governments participating in the Fourth World Conference on Women,
2. Gathered here in Beijing in September 1995, the year of the fiftieth anniversary of the founding of the United Nations,
3. Determined to advance the goals of equality, development and peace for all women everywhere in the interest of all humanity,
4. Acknowledging the voices of all women everywhere and taking note of the diversity of women and their roles and circumstances, honoring the women who paved the way and inspired by the hope present in the world's youth,
5. Recognize that the status of women has advanced in some important respects in the past decade but that progress has been uneven, inequalities between women and men have persisted and major obstacles remain, with serious consequences for the well-being of all people,
6. Also recognize that this situation is exacerbated by the increasing poverty that is affecting the lives of the majority of the world's people, in particular women and children, with origins in both the national and international domains,

7. Dedicate ourselves unreservedly to addressing these constraints and obstacles and thus enhancing further the advancement and empowerment of women all over the world, and agree that this requires urgent action in the spirit of determination, hope, cooperation and solidarity, now and to carry us forward into the next century.

We reaffirm our commitment to:

8. The equal rights and inherent human dignity of women and men and other purposes and principles enshrined in the Charter of the United Nations, to the Universal Declaration of Human Rights and other international human rights instruments, in particular the Convention on the Elimination of All Forms of Discrimination against Women and the Convention on the Rights of the Child, as well as the Declaration on the Elimination of Violence against Women and the Declaration on the Right to Development;
9. Ensure the full implementation of the human rights of women and of the girl child as an inalienable, integral and indivisible part of all human rights and fundamental freedoms;
10. Build on consensus and progress made at previous United Nations Conferences and summits—on women in Nairobi in 1985, on children in New York in 1990, on environment and development in Rio de Janeiro in1992, on human rights in Vienna in 1993, on population and development in Cairo in 1994 and on social development in Copenhagen in 1995 with the objective of achieving equality, development and peace;
11. Achieve the full and effective implementation of the Nairobi Forward-looking Strategies for the Advancement of Women;
12. The empowerment and advancement of women, including the right to freedom of thought, conscience, religion and belief, thus contributing to the moral, ethical, spiritual and

intellectual needs of women and men, individually or in community with others and thereby guaranteeing them the possibility of realizing their full potential in society and shaping their lives in accordance with their own aspirations.

We are convinced that:

13. Women's empowerment and their full participation on the basis of equality in all spheres of society, including participation in the decision-making process and access to power, are fundamental for the achievement of equality, development and peace;
14. Women's rights are human rights;
15. Equal rights, opportunities and access to resources, equal sharing of responsibilities for the family by men and women, and a harmonious partnership between them are critical to their well-being and that of their families as well as to the consolidation of democracy;
16. Eradication of poverty based on sustained economic growth, social development, environmental protection and social justice requires the involvement of women in economic and social development, equal opportunities and the full and equal participation of women and men as agents and beneficiaries of people-centred sustainable development;
17. The explicit recognition and reaffirmation of the right of all women to control all aspects of their health, in particular their own fertility, is basic to their empowerment;
18. Local, national, regional and global peace is attainable and is inextricably linked with the advancement of women, who are a fundamental force for leadership, conflict resolution and the promotion of lasting peace at all levels;
19. It is essential to design, implement and monitor, with the full participation of women, effective, efficient and mutually reinforcing gender-sensitive policies and programmes, including development policies and programmes, at all

levels that will foster the empowerment and advancement of women;

20. The participation and contribution of all actors of civil society, particularly women's groups and networks and other non-governmental organizations and community-based organizations, with full respect for their autonomy, in cooperation with Governments, are important to the effective implementation and follow-up of the Platform for Action;
21. The implementation of the Platform for Action requires commitment from Governments and the international community. By making national and international commitments for action, including those made at the Conference, Governments and the international community recognize the need to take priority action for the empowerment and advancement of women.

We are determined to:

22. Intensify efforts and actions to achieve the goals of the Nairobi Forward-looking Strategies for the Advancement of Women by the end of this century;
23. Ensure the full enjoyment by women and the girl child of all human rights and fundamental freedoms and take effective action against violations of these rights and freedoms;
24. Take all necessary measures to eliminate all forms of discrimination against women and the girl child and remove all obstacles to gender equality and the advancement and empowerment of women;
25. Encourage men to participate fully in all actions towards equality;
26. Promote women's economic independence, including employment, and eradicate the persistent and increasing burden of poverty on women by addressing the structural causes of poverty through changes uneconomic, ensuring equal access for all women, including those in rural areas,

as vital development agents, to productive resources, opportunities and public services;

27. Promote people-centred sustainable development, including sustained economic growth, through the provision of basic education, life-long education, literacy and training, and primary health care for girls and women;
28. Take positive steps to ensure peace for the advancement of women and, recognizing the leading role that women have played in the peace movement, work actively towards general and complete disarmament under strict and effective international control, and support negotiations on the conclusion, without delay, of a universal and multilaterally and effectively verifiable comprehensive nuclear-test-ban treaty which contributes to nuclear disarmament and the prevention of the proliferation of nuclear weapons in all its aspects;
29. Prevent and eliminate all forms of violence against women and girls;
30. Ensure equal access to and equal treatment of women and men in education and health care and enhance women's sexual and reproductive health as well as education;
31. Promote and protect all human rights of women and girls;
32. Intensify efforts to ensure equal enjoyment of all human rights and fundamental freedoms for all women and girls who face multiple barriers to their empowerment and advancement because of such factors as their race, age, language, ethnicity, culture, religion, or disability, or because they are indigenous people;
33. Ensure respect for international law, including humanitarian law, in order to protect women and girls in particular;
34. Develop the fullest potential of girls and women of all ages, ensure their full and equal participation in building a better world for all and enhance their role in the development process.

We are determined to:

35. Ensure women's equal access to economic resources, including land, credit, science and technology, vocational training, information, communication and markets, as a means to further the advancement and empowerment of women and girls, including through the enhancement of their capacities to enjoy the benefits of equal access to these resources, *inter alia*, by means of international cooperation;
36. Ensure the success of the Platform for Action, which will require a strong commitment on the part of Governments, international organizations and institutions at all levels. We are deeply convinced that economic development, social development and environmental protection are interdependent and mutually reinforcing components of sustainable development, which is the framework for our efforts to achieve a higher quality of life for all people. Equitable social development that recognizes empowering the poor, particularly women living in poverty, to utilize environmental resources sustainably is a necessary foundation for sustainable development. We also recognize that broad-based and sustained economic growth in the context of sustainable development is necessary to sustain social development and social justice. The success of the Platform for Action will also require adequate mobilization of resources at the national and international levels as well as new and additional resources to the developing countries from all available funding mechanisms, including multilateral, bilateral and private sources for the advancement of women; financial resources to strengthen the capacity of national, sub-regional, regional and international institutions; a commitment to equal rights, equal responsibilities and equal opportunities and to the equal participation of women and men in all national, regional and international bodies and policy-making processes; and the establishment or

strengthening of mechanisms at all levels for accountability to the world's women;

37. Ensure also the success of the Platform for Action in countries with economies in transition, which will require continued international cooperation and assistance;
38. We hereby adopt and commit ourselves as Governments to implement the following Platform for Action, ensuring that a gender perspectives reflected in all our policies and programmes. We urge the United Nations system, regional and international financial institutions, other relevant regional and international institutions and all women and men, as well as non-governmental organizations, with full respect for their autonomy, and all sectors of civil society, in cooperation with Governments, to fully commit themselves and contribute to the implementation of this Platform for Action.

Bibliography

Books

Annual Report of NCPCR.

Bedprakas Syam Roy (2019). *India's Approach towards Sustainable Development Goals*, Kalpaz Publications, New Delhi.

______(2021). *The Impact of Climate Change on Sustainable Developments with Reference to India*, New Delhi Publishers, New Delhi.

Indian Penal Code (IPC) 1860.

Social Statistics Division, Ministry of Statistics and Programme Implementation, Government of India (2016): *Disabled Persons in India, A Statistical Profile 2016.*

UNDP Human Development Report 2020.

Articles

Braithwaite, J. and Mont, D. (2009). Disability and poverty: a Survey of World Bank Poverty Assessments and implications, Alter, *European Journal of Disability Research*, pp. 219-32.

Mitra, Sophie (2006). The Capability Approach and Disability, *Journal of Disability Policy Studies,* Vol. 16, No. 4, pp. 236-47.

______(2013): A data revolution for disability-inclusive development, *The Lancet Global Health*, Vol. 1, Issue 4, October 1, PE178-E179.

_______(2013). A data revolution for disability-inclusive development (downloaded from https://www.thelancet.com/action/showPdf?pii=S2214-109X%2813%2970016-0 on 30.10.2019)

Mitra, S. and Sambamoorthi, U. (2009): Wage differential by disability status in an agrarian labour market in India, *Applied Economics Letters*, Taylor & Francis.

Teresa Njoroge Mwendwa Ambrose Murangira Raymond Lang (June 2009): Mainstreaming the rights of persons with disabilities in national development frameworks, https://doi.org/10.1002/jid.1594

Vulnerable tribes: lost in a classification trap—*The Hindu* Address: https://www.thehindu.com/news/national/vulnerable-tribes-lost-in-a-classification-trap/article17894997.eceDate visited: 26 June 2019.

WHO, The World Bank. *World Report on Disability*. Geneva: World Health Organization, 2011.

Websites

Census of India, 2011.

Child Budget of India.

Constitution of India—11th and 12th Schedules of the Constitution of India.

Convention of the Child Rights, 1989.

Elderly in India 2021, Government of India.

First World Conference on Women in Mexico, 1975.

Fourth World Conference on Women in Beijing, 1995.

Gender Budget in India.

Global Gender Gap Report Posted On: 17 Dec 2021 3:15PM by PIB Delhi.

Gyan Pathak: The Meghalaya Editorial, February 21, 2023.

High-Level Political Forum on Sustainable Development—sustainabledevelopment.un.org/hlpf/2019

http://www.disabilityaffairs.gov.in/upload/uploadfiles/files/disabilityinindia2011data.pdf http://disabilityaffairs.gov.in/

content/page/state-ut-wise-persons.php www. Indiastat.com Sustainable Development Summit Declaration, September 2015.

India Index and Dashboard 2020-21.

Kiran Pandey: *India's SDG Preparedness: ranking continues to decline*, 6th June, 2022.

Legislations on Women in India.

National Commission for Protection of Child Rights.

National Family Health Surveys 2005-06 and 2015-16.

National Policy on Older Persons—C.P. Sujaya

National Policy for Older Persons Year 1999, Ministry of Social Justice and Empowerment, Government of India, Shastri Bhawan, New Delhi.

NCPCR Act, 2005.

NFHS-5.

NITI Aayog and the SDGs in India.

Policy for the Aged: Opportunities and Challenges—National Institute of Rural Development & Panchayati Raj, Hyderabad.

Right to Education Act, 2009.

Second World Conference on Women in Copenhegan, 1980.

The 5Ps of the Sustainable Development Goals—the_5ps_of_the_sustainable_development_goals_pdf, Sustainable Knowledge Forum

The Global Child Report, 2020.

The Global Gender Gap 2022, Report of the WEP.

The Status of the World of Children Report 2021/2020/2019.

The Status of Gender Budgeting in India—Ria Kasliwal, 23 December, 2021.

The UN Sustainable Development Goals Report, 2022.

Third World Conference on Women in Nairobi, 1985.

Tribal Welfare at a glance, May 2014, Ministry of Tribal Welfare, Government of India, National Commission for Scheduled Tribes, Statewise PTGs List from MTA.pdf Address: http://www.ncst.nic.in/sites/default/files/documents/StatewisePTGsList%20from%20MTA.pdf (Date visited: 26 June, 2019).

U.N. Charter 3. UN General Assembly Resolution 1975.

UN Sustainable Development Summit Declaration 2015.

Various Legislations on Children Rights of India.

Voluntary National Review (VNR) at UN's High-Level Political Forum 2020.

Website of the NITI Aayog, Government of India.

Index